THE
PLAIN AND SIMPLE
GUIDE
TO
Music
PUBLISHING

by Randall D. Wixen

HAL•LEONARD®

ISBN-13: 978-0-634-09054-7
ISBN-10: 0-634-09054-2

Published by Hal Leonard Corporation
7777 W. Bluemound Road
P.O. Box 13819
Milwaukee, WI 53213

Hal Leonard books are available at your local bookstore, or you may order through Music Dispatch at 1-800-637-2852 or www.musicdispatch.com.

Library of Congress Cataloging-in-Publication Data

Wixen, Randall D.
   The plain and simple guide to music publishing / Randall D. Wixen.--1st. ed.
      p. cm.
   Includes index.
   ISBN 0-634-09054-2
   1. Music publishing--United States. 2. Copyright--Music. 3. Music--Economic aspects. I. Title
ML112.W58 2005
070.5'794'0973--dc22
                         2005007037

Printed in the U.S.A.

First Edition

Visit Hal Leonard Online at **www.halleonard.com**

Contents

Foreword

In the early '70s my bandmates and I arrived in Los Angeles, fresh and green, and within days of shopping our demo tape up and down Sunset Boulevard we were offered deals with three different big-time record labels. Just old enough to get ourselves into some real legal trouble, my pals and I went for the deal with the most money up front. A staggering $10,000. No small sum to us in those days, plus there was talk of buying us new amplifiers, and oh, first we had to sign something called a publishing agreement. This came up as we stood pen in hand around the desk, all set to close the deal of a lifetime.

We had no manager, which didn't seem to upset the label, who advised us we might need a lawyer to go over the contracts. We had found one with no trouble on the recommendation of a bass player we knew in Topanga Canyon. But publishing was something that hadn't really come up in our discussions. The lawyer had seen a quick thousand bucks and told us things looked good to him, so understandably there were some quiet stares between us as we sized up this deal-or-no-deal situation. Hell, why hold this thing up over publishing? Let 'em print the songbooks . . . So we all signed, and drinks were lifted.

Thirty years later, after throwing countless dollar bills at shaky lawyers, some of that deal still sticks to my feet. You may ask, "Who is he to complain?" and you might be right. It's true that after many a well-publicized lawsuit I was able to regain my publishing rights and have had a wonderful and lucrative career in music. But to this day I do not own the copyrights to my first few records. The record company went out of business, and through some spin of the wheel

I wound up owning the actual master tapes. But the sacred publishing remains something that can't be bought. How could this happen? It's simple. I didn't have Randall Wixen's book! Hell, in the '50s, the writer of a book like this might have been dropped in a lake with concrete shoes.

Check the shelves: even today, you'll find precious little of this information made simple for the guy on the street. Why? Because music publishing is still one of the greatest scams for ripping off an artist ever created. I am far from alone in having to pay the price of an education in the music business.

You'd be hard pressed to find a songwriter without a similar tale of woe or one far worse. I once attended an ASCAP awards dinner and was fascinated to see, time after time, six people go up and take a bow for a song one guy wrote. To the man on the street it must be hard to imagine how something that is so personal and intangible can be wrestled away from the poor fellow who was humming something in his head, to become a stream of income for countless shysters, corporations, managers, and ex-wives. But yes, my friend, as you will read in these pages, this is often what happens.

It has been my pleasure to know this book's author for many a happy year of him managing my two publishing companies (as he does for a number of writers I have great respect for). And I always feel sure he'll track down every penny on B sides only released in Guam. Randall Wixen is that rare man of integrity in a business that I'm not gonna call crooked, but I'm not gonna call it anything else. Anyway, here's a chance to learn how to own those random inspirations that cross your mind, and a book that could be the most valuable writing partner you'll ever hook up with.

Enjoy,

Tom Petty

Acknowledgments

To Adam Holzman who, in the summer of 1967 at Tumbleweed Day Camp, actually knew the Doors and got me interested in the music business;

To my neighbor and friend George Braunstein, who was in the music business and let me work with him and his bands as I was growing up;

To Joe Nolte and Vitus Matare, who let me manage their band, the Last;

To James Young from Styx, who believed in me and introduced me to Bernie Gudvi;

To Bernie Gudvi, who brought me up to the majors;

To Buddha, Cree, and Jackson, and to Tom Petty and Tony Dimitriades, for their friendship, support, and moral guidance throughout the years;

To Michael Jensen, who urged me write this book, to Roger McNamee for giving me his detailed thoughts on the first draft manuscript, to Jeffrey Pepper Rodgers for his insightful comments and editing, to the folks at Hal Leonard for publishing it, and to Michael Hamilburg for helping me sell it;

To everyone else who I've inadvertently omitted and who helped inspire me with their encouragement, discouragement, and/or ineptitude throughout the years;

To Sharon, who didn't want me to be an actuarial technician for PennCorp Financial even if it meant giving up that $1,270 a month salary, and to my amazing boys, Andrew and Jonny . . .

Thank you.

Introduction

Remember the story of the emperor's new clothes? It's a fable about a haughty and vain emperor who commissions some phony tailors to make some very expensive clothes for him. The swindlers charge the emperor a small fortune, deliver an empty hanger upon which, they say, hangs clothes that only the worthiest of people can see, and quickly make their way out of town. Rather than show that he is unworthy and cannot see what isn't there, the emperor puts on the imaginary new clothes and parades through the streets. Only a guile-free young child admits that there is nothing to see and remarks that the leader is, in fact, naked.

Well, the music business is full of naked emperors, and because I deal with them all day long, I get frustrated. I am continually amazed at the number of people I meet who hold the highest positions in the record and publishing industries yet know so little of the actual mechanics of the business. These people have attained their positions through force of personality, personal relationships, a little bit of knowledge, leveraging positions of trust, lateral moves from other businesses and firms, and various other (sometimes nefarious) means that don't constitute optimal qualification. It is truly rare that I meet people who actually know what they should know and are well qualified for the positions they hold.

With some frequency I get phone calls from managers of multiplatinum acts who want to know what a 3% producer's royalty means in dollars and cents, or from lawyers who want to know what normal industry terms are for various types of deals. Imagine negotiating multimillion-dollar deals knowing only that 4% is better than 3% but without a clue about the inner mechanics about how residuals are calculated.

I'm convinced that one manager I know is so dumb that he can only, and just barely, count to ten. So why is he so successful? I guess because whichever of his ten numbers he uses when negotiating a deal, he always remembers to authoritatively and convincingly speak it followed by the words "million dollars."

This kind of ignorance doesn't fly so well, though, in the current business environment of mergers, acquisitions, copyright theft, and downsizing. Those who actually know something (and sometimes, unfortunately, those who are simply cheaper naked emperors) are the ones who seem likely to be running tomorrow's music companies.

But what makes me so smart that I can judge my fellow industry "professionals" as being dumb and unworthy of their positions? Who decreed that I am the one who actually knows something? Am I just another guy who thinks he knows more than he does?

I started my music business education in the middle and late 1970s while I was attending Palisades High School in Los Angeles. I worked after school and on the weekends for one of my parents' neighbors, who struck it big as a personal manager. I got to answer fan letters and fill out BMI forms. I didn't get paid, but I learned a lot and got to hang out backstage and in recording studios.

I started managing bands myself during high school and throughout college. But with personal management, I rapidly discovered that I was too Type A in this loose and creative world, often frustrated by musicians who couldn't show up for that 4 P.M. interview or remember to pick up a guitar cable before a gig. So I soon moved on to where I was most comfortable and useful, which was in the business aspects as the behind-the-scenes worker bee.

My formal educational background consists of a degree in economics from UCLA, where I was the music editor of *The Daily Bruin*; several professional postgraduate courses in the fine points of music publishing, song plugging, and international business law; and attendance at music business conventions, meetings, and seminars throughout the world. Locally, I have attended meetings at the California Copyright Conference and the Association of Independent Music Publishers, among others.

For many years I have read voraciously on the subject of music business affairs and copyright law, both in periodicals and in books. Some of my favorites are *This Business of Music* by M. William Krasilovsky and Sidney Shemel (Billboard Books), which I discovered on a shelf as a teenager while babysitting for an entertainment attorney's children, and, more recently, Donald S. Passman's *All You Need to Know About the Music Business* (Simon & Schuster).

Although I never went to law school, I've nonetheless been published by the local bar association and have often been asked to provide expert testimony in copyright cases. And while I never went to a business school or through an MBA program, I am frequently sought as a guest lecturer at trade associations and at major universities.

Today, I am the primary owner of a music publishing administration company based in the Los Angeles area (Calabasas). We employ 15 people who handle about 900 accounts, and our artist roster includes many of the top songwriters of the last 50 years. Our clientele and catalog is the envy of firms ten times our size. Our specialty is a highly detail-oriented approach to publishing administration, and we find and recover lots of unpaid and underpaid royalties every year. One attorney we know called us the "most anal-retentive group of people I have ever known," and we wear those words as a badge of pride.

So those are my credentials.

What finally pushed me over the edge and got me started on this book was a recent conversation with a singer-songwriter who has sold millions of records throughout the world. He kept talking about the mechanical royalties, and I assumed he knew what the term meant. But it ultimately came out that he thought, mistakenly, that mechanical royalties were his artist royalties. For five minutes we'd been talking about completely different things—the issue he was concerned about was not the same issue I was advising on.

This book was written, therefore, to put the necessary information out there in an easily absorbed form. I want to help musicians, songwriters, industry professionals, and even naked emperors acquire the knowledge that they want and really should have. I want this book to be a user-friendly, generalist's guide to music publishing, and not a comprehensively technical treatise on the subject. I want the book to be readable, interesting, and sometimes humorous—not just a dry dump of information. But I also want it to have enough depth that it is actually useful and not just an overview. I will try to keep the discussion and the examples simple enough that they are understandable to those who forget that 4 P.M. interview and their guitar cord, but with sufficient depth and detail to be useful to those either working in the music business or aspiring to be in it.

Almost everyone who has a career in the music business, especially artists who record their own songs, will tell you how important publishing is. Recording artists can run up huge debts to their labels for things like advances, tour support, recording costs, video costs, equipment, and the like. It is not uncommon for even highly successful artists to owe hundreds of thousands (even millions) of dollars to their labels over long periods of time. By contrast, publishing income is almost never recoupable from recording artist royalties and advances, so songs and publishing rights generate income that starts coming in as soon as the first copy of your record is sold.

For many musicians, financial stability and an economically viable career are only possible via the songwriting and publishing income that is generated while their recording artist accounts are miserable bottomless pits. The adage "Don't give up your publishing" is as important and true today as it ever was. If you sell everything you've got, you don't have anything left to make money off of or sell. Most seasoned recording artists who write songs will tell you how keeping their publishing rights was the most important thing they ever did, or otherwise they'll tell you how selling their songs was the worst mistake they ever made. And songs have economic lives that extend way beyond the time when the album they were originally on disappears from the charts.

The subjects of music publishing, what publishers do, and how they should best do it contain many areas that are subject to personal opinions and preferences. My opinions are liberally interspersed with hard facts throughout the book, and I will do my best to be clear about which is which. I write as the owner of an independent music publishing administration firm and not from the perspective of a music rights licenser, a record company, or a publishing house that owns or co-owns copyrights. Ideologically, I believe that writers should retain their own copyrights and control them closely, and that alliances with multinational music publishing firms are rarely in the writers' best interests. You have been thus advised.

My hope is that anything not covered in this book will be a fairly specific or detailed issue that requires expert consultation or in-depth research. If you make it through the book and absorb its contents, you might be missing a sock but you won't be naked anymore.

Overview

What is music publishing? Not what it sounds like. The term suggests the publishing and printing of sheet music, but in fact, this is only a very small part of what music publishers actually do.

Music publishing is the owning and exploiting of musical copyrights. There are many types of *rights* within a *copyright* that can be exploited. One can license the reproduction of sound recordings such as CDs, tapes, and records. One can license public performance of a song. Songs may be *synchronized* in timed relation with visual images in movies and television shows and in DVD and VHS programs. They can be incorporated into advertising, karaoke programs, telephone ringtones, samples, MIDI sequences, piano rolls, greeting cards, toys, video games, Internet uses, and more. And, of course, songs can also be exploited and sold as sheet music.

The music publisher controls all of these rights. Additionally, in almost all instances other than the licensing of sound recordings embodying a publisher's song (where special *compulsory* provisions may apply), the publisher has the legal right to grant a license, or forego a license, for a particular use. In these instances, the publisher also gets the right to determine the license fee or royalty rate received through negotiations with the final user. In short, music publishers are really *rights holders* and *licensers* and not primarily people with printing presses.

The control and licensing of compositions is a unique responsibility. Great care must be taken to determine which uses are appropriate for a given song and what fees should be charged. A long-term view must be incorporated into this analysis, and a particular license request must be weighed against the effects that the use will have on the song. For example, licensing a critically prestigious work to a television dog-food commercial for $100,000 would certainly make the publisher $100,000, but it would likely have negative long-term effects on other licenses and uses. Such a commercial, if well known and frequently shown, would in all likelihood make other artists less likely to make new recordings of the song and would also probably eliminate synchronization uses (i.e., the song in synchronism with pictures, as in films and TV shows). In other words, neither recording artists nor film and television producers would be as interested in using a song with strong dog-food associations in the mind of the general public. Accordingly, care in decision making results in the long-term health of a musical copyright.

Copyright Basics

Under United States copyright law, a musical work is protected by law and inures to the benefit of the authors once it has been "fixed in a tangible medium from which it may be reproduced." This means once a writer records the work into a media from which it can be reproduced in his or her absence, it is copyrighted. Examples of this *fixing* would be writing down words and notes on a piece of paper, singing a melody and words into a cassette recorder, embodying the song in some sort of computer file, or even developing a notation language and putting notches on a stick. The only requirement is that given the proper playback instructions or mechanisms, someone can reproduce the essence of your song.

The filing of a completed copyright form along with a copy of the work fixed in a *tangible medium* with the U.S. Copyright Office is a formality with many significant benefits. But the failure to do so does not mean that an author loses ownership of the copyright and the rights attendant thereto. Your copyright exists from the instant you "fix it" by putting it onto paper, tape, sticks, etc.

Registering your works does give you additional rights as a copyright owner. Registration is required, for example, before you can institute a copyright infringement suit in a federal court. But there is no time limit for registering a work after its creation. So if you wrote a song 25 years ago and never registered it with the

Copyright Office, and someone just got a tape of it and put it in a film without your permission, you could presently register the song and then sue for infringement. But if your evil brother-in-law Smedley copyrighted the song 20 years ago without your knowledge, listing himself as the owner and writer, then you'd have a hard (but not necessarily impossible) time convincing a court that you are the rightful owner and claimant, and entitled to damages and other compensation from the film company.

Registration of a work constitutes *prima facie* evidence that you are the owner. Prima facie evidence is a little like a deed to your property registered with the county recorder. You might actually own the property, but registering the deed or your claim with the county gives official public notice to your claim. Such registration is pretty strong evidence that you make the claim to the property, but again, if someone wrongly registered a deed to your property in his own name with the local county recorder, you could still take legal action to show that such recordation was fraudulently made. Given the benefits versus the costs of recordation (both for deeds and copyrights), it is highly advisable to take this step.

Songs are registered in the U.S. Copyright Office on what is called a *PA copyright* form. PA stands for performing arts and includes not only musical works but dramatic works (such as scripts and videotaped improvisations), dance choreography, motion pictures, and other audiovisual works. The charge for a PA copyright is currently $30 and also requires that a deposit be made of the work as fixed in its tangible medium. So you send in $30, a completed PA form, and a tape or CD of you singing your soon-to-be-hit song, and eventually the Copyright Office will send you back a copyright certificate with the Copyright Office seal on it.

Two Types of Copyrights

An important distinction must be made at this point. There exists another type of copyright, an *SR copyright*, which is used to copyright sound recordings. According to the Copyright Office: "Sound recordings are 'works that result from the fixation of a series of musical, spoken, or other sounds, but not including the sounds accompanying a motion picture or other audiovisual work.' Common examples include recordings of music, drama, or lectures."

It is extremely important that you grasp the difference between PA and SR copyrights at this point, or the rest of this book will lack proper meaning. Let's take two scenarios.

You are the Beatles. (Congratulations on your fine career!) You have just recorded "Twist and Shout" by Phil Medley and Bert Russell. The music publishers of "Twist and Shout" own the PA copyright. That is, they own the composition itself. Your record label registers an SR copyright of you, the Beatles, doing the song. *This SR copyright does not cover the composition "Twist and Shout," but only your performing elements within this recording, such as your singing and playing of instruments.* The PA copyright in the underlying composition is still owned and controlled by Medley's and Russell's publishers.

Likewise, your contemporaries such as Tom Jones and the Isley Brothers, who are also recording this great song, have labels that are themselves obtaining SR copyrights in their artists' particular recordings of the song.

In general, then, there is only one PA copyright for the underlying composition, but there may be any number of SR copyrights corresponding to different master recordings. (In some cases multiple PA copyrights may be filed: for instance, for a work in its published and unpublished forms, or for marching band and classical guitar arrangements of a song.)

So, Beatles, your record label now needs to pay for two sets of rights. The label has to pay the owners of the PA copyright for "Twist and Shout" for the use of their song on records publicly distributed, and it also has to pay for the right to embody the SR copyright master recording on those same records. In other words, the label must pay for the use of the underlying composition (PA), and must pay you too for your singing and playing (SR). Copyrights in songs are shown as "© 2004 Joe Schmoe Music" and copyrights in sound recordings are shown as "℗ 2004 Rippemoff Records."

Mechanical Royalties

The fee payable for the use of the underlying composition (the PA copyright) is called a *mechanical royalty*. The mechanical royalty is fixed at a *statutory rate* in the United States, that is, at a rate that is fixed by statute, or law. At the time of publication, the statutory rate for a song whose performance is under five minutes in length is 8.5¢ per copy distributed. The mechanical royalty that a publisher accepts may also be negotiated downward by the record company offering the publisher additional incentives such as advances. Such reductions are entirely a matter of negotiation between the publisher and mechanical user, and will be discussed at greater length in later chapters.

The fees payable to you mop tops by your label for your particular master recording (the SR copyright) are not governed by statute but by the terms of your negotiated recording agreement. These are generally called *artist royalties* but are on occasion referred to as *master license royalties* or *recording royalties*. For consistency's sake, we will refer to these payments in this book as artist royalties. (Mechanical royalties, too, are sometimes referred to as copyright royalties, but I prefer not to use this convention because, as explained above, there are different types of copyright royalties.) In general, the current practice is that artist royalties are paid based on a percentage of the wholesale or retail selling price of the recording, whether it is in CD, tape, Internet delivery, or other form. Additionally, you as a recording artist may even elect to waive royalties altogether and do your recording for a flat fee or on a *work-for-hire* basis.

So we can see that both the writers and the recording artists get paid, and in separate and different ways. Now let's look at a second scenario.

You're still the Beatles, but now you've written a song called "Something." What changes? Not much really, except that you're now wearing two hats. You're the recording artist and you still get your artist royalties. But even though you've written the song yourself, your record label still has an obligation to pay mechanical royalties for the use of the underlying composition you've written. In this instance, such mechanical license and payment will be made to George Harrison's publishing company.

A few additional words of note on mechanical royalties. First, generally speaking, record labels must pay mechanical royalties to you for each and every record they distribute. Usual industry standard and practice is that no costs or advances are deducted from mechanical royalties, and that mechanical royalties are payable to you from the first record the label distributes onward. Artist royalties, on the other hand, are more typically recouped by the record label against the recording and other costs that it has advanced to you. For example, if the label gave you an advance of $25,000, the first $25,000 your record earns in artist royalties goes to pay back the label. Recording artists typically must earn back large balances before they start making money from a record, while publishers of songs on that same record are in the black from record one.

Performance Royalties

Let's move on now and discuss another type of publishing royalty, the *performance royalty*.

Performance royalties (and the underlying performance license) relate to the performance of your song in public. The performance of your song may be made in many ways and for many different types of benefits. The two most common types of public performance are performance of your song on radio or TV. Radio and TV stations like to perform your works because it helps them attract listeners and viewers, which in turn helps them to sell advertising.

Some other public performers of music (who must therefore license said rights) are restaurants, nightclubs, bars, aerobic studios, airlines with movie and/or TV services, kiddie gyms, schools, clothing boutiques, stores, telephone hold music services, elevator and environmental music providers, and concert venues.

Performance royalties may be licensed directly to a user by a publisher. However, the general practice of music publishers is to authorize an organization specializing in performing rights to license public performance of their works. The two biggest organizations that license music performing rights in the United States are ASCAP and BMI. ASCAP and BMI are not themselves publishers. Their function, and how they work to license and collect performing rights income for music publishers, will be discussed at greater length in a separate chapter.

Synchronization

Another significant source of income for music publishers is the *synchronization fee* or *royalty*. Synchronization occurs when a musical work is synchronized in timed, linear relation with visual images. Examples of this are background, theme, and featured uses of music in motion pictures and television shows. The producer or director might feel that music would enhance the impact of certain scenes or drama within the program. Pre-existing music is often licensed for this purpose and may include current hit or classic songs. Likewise, the producer or director might make arrangements with a composer to write music specifically for the production. Typically, pre-existing music is done on a license basis, while music specifically written to be a part of a production is done on a *work-for-hire* (or flat fee) basis, although there are occasional exceptions to these practices.

Just as we distinguished between artist royalties and mechanical royalties when discussing records earlier in this chapter, we must make similar distinctions here. A film producer requires two analogous sets of rights to put music in his film. First he must *clear* publishing rights from the publisher. Clearing publishing from the publisher (PA copyright) is also sometimes (more confusingly perhaps) referred to as a *sync* or *synchronization license*.

The film producer must also clear the right to use a particular master recording (SR copyright) within the film or, alternatively, create a master recording specifically for the film. To use our example from above, the production must obtain a publishing sync license for "Twist and Shout" from Medley's and Russell's publishers, *and* it must obtain rights to use a particular recording of the song. This *master license* might be for the master recording made by the Beatles, Tom Jones, or the Isley Brothers, or it may be explicitly commissioned and created by the production specifically for that film, and perhaps the corresponding soundtrack album. It is traditional, although by no means required, that such payments are made on a flat fee (as opposed to royalty) basis and that the publisher's sync fee is usually the same amount as the master license fee.

Synchronization licenses (except in rare instances discussed in the later chapter on synchronizations) may be declined by the publisher; for example, perhaps the publisher doesn't want the song in an X-rated movie or in *Rambo 13*. The publisher may also limit such licenses to a specific type of use (film festivals only, for example) or for a specific period of time (five years only, for example). Likewise, the license may be incredibly far reaching, covering all uses within the program through "the Universe," for the entire life of copyright and any and all renewals, in corresponding advertising and promotions, on home video devices, and in any other media "now known or hereinafter devised." The range of synchronization licenses and terms is broad indeed.

Another important point to remember about synchronization licensing is that a synchronization use and a public performance are different things and involve different licenses and rights. Just because a producer licenses a song you have written to be synchronized with his TV show or film, it doesn't follow that a TV station or airline has the right to publicly perform your work for its financial (or other) benefit. Even though you allowed the producer to put your song in his sitcom, CBS TV must still obtain public performing rights for the broadcast of the program in which the song was synchronized. While this may seem like double-dipping, it really is not. It is simply the case of the two users of your music (the sitcom producer and the TV station) paying their own shares of the total rights needed for the broadcast. The producer needs only synchronization rights, and the TV station only needs the performance rights, so the producer does not obtain all rights needed to broadcast the show onto television sets everywhere but shifts this financial burden to its rightful place—the TV station. The producer gets no direct benefit from the TV broadcast, as he does not get to sell advertising for the broadcast, so he makes the TV stations pay for the public performing rights out of their advertising and other revenue. (An example of "other revenue" would be HBO, which earns money not from advertising but from monthly fees charged to end viewers.)

A final peculiarity of copyright law in the United States that bears mentioning is the fact that we have no performance license or royalty for over-the-air broadcasts payable to the owners of master recordings. (Most of Europe and some other parts of the world are different—organizations such as PPL and GVL do collect performing rights for master owners and recording artists.) So, if that sitcom that we were just talking about gets performed on TV, and if that sitcom embodies a pre-existing master recording, there will be no additional performing right fee paid to the owner of the master recording. While a publisher gets both a synchronization fee from a producer, and performing right royalties from ASCAP or BMI for the public performance of a song in a sitcom or other production, the master recording owner (unless the master was created as a work for hire) only receives a master license fee for the synchronization of the master recording and gets *no* performance royalty.

Two recent U.S. laws have made things a little more fair. The Digital Performance in Sound Recordings Act of 1995 and the Digital Millenium Copyright Act of 1998 grant a performing right for sound recordings made via digital transmissions, such as over the Internet or for electronic subscription services. An organization called SoundExchange administers and collects these performing royalties.

Other Types of Income

There are various other types of licensing and income for music publishers. While not typically as financially important to music publishers, these other licenses can, on occasion, be very significant. Within the printed music realm, such uses would include sheet music, matching album folios, lyric books, and

Internet downloading of printed music. Karaoke uses and cellular telephone ringtones can generate supplemental licensing and revenue. The creation of a *derivative work*—for instance, the sampling or interpolation of musical elements from a pre-existing song, or foreign-language lyrics being set to an existing melody—may lead to additional use of a song. Video games are becoming a place where many songs are used and placed for profit. And technology continues to advance at a pace where important uses of music of which we have not yet conceived may become common-place before we know it.

Songwriters and Publishers

Up until now, except when you were busy being the Beatles, we've pretty much ignored the crucial element in music publishing: the creator of the song. Songwriters are often the most overlooked players in the whole process. You can talk business all day long, but if no one wrote the song, there is no mechanical license, no performing right, no synchronization, and no cellular ringtone. It all starts with the songwriter.

In the old days, and more or less up until the end of the Brill Building era in the 1960s, songwriters were rarely the same people who popularized the songs. Irving Berlin would write a song, and then Al Jolson would record and otherwise popularize it. Arthur Crudup would write "That's Alright Mama," and then Elvis would have a hit with it.

In those days, a songwriter would affiliate with a music publisher, whose job was to get someone to record the song, or popularize it on Broadway or in a touring vaudeville show. The music publisher took a very active role in taking the song and then creating an economic value for it by doing what was then called *song plugging* (now frequently referred to as *professional* or *active* activity). The writer and the publisher were partners in the venture, and thus was born a traditional 50/50 split of income between the music publisher and the songwriter. The music publisher may have owned the entire song, but the writer got half of the money that the music publisher was able to collect from the users. (A slight exception to this generalization involving the treatment of performance income will be discussed in the later chapter on performance income.)

The true end of the traditional publisher/songwriter relationship and arrangement came with the advent of singers who wrote their own songs. Most notably, this was at the beginning of the 1960s when people like Bob Dylan and the Beatles started writing their own songs and putting them on their own records. Fingers started scratching heads as these artists wondered why it was necessary to split half the publishing money with a music publisher who was no longer fulfilling the traditional publisher role of getting the songs recorded and doing the work to make them popular. The new singer-songwriters were completing both functions (the writing and the popularizing) on their own and became reticent to receive only half of the proceeds for doing almost all of the work.

Many singer-songwriters moved to abandon the traditional relationship with music publishers and to start their own music publishing companies. With their own companies they could better control the use of their songs and keep a greater share of the income in a more proper balance to their efforts. Publishing administrators and other people and companies with similar knowledge would be paid relatively nominal fees to handle the business aspects of running the publishing company, issuing the licenses, and collecting the income. The songwriter, then, became both the writer and the publisher of the songs and retained the lion's share of the revenue and control, and it became much rarer for publishers to play their traditional role in plugging the music.

The traditional writer/publisher relationship still does exist and can be seen, albeit far less frequently, with artists who are not known primarily as songwriters (Barbra Streisand and Celine Dion, for example) and in quarters where the music producer (analogous to a film director) exerts greater influence, such as in the Nashville music scene. Country artists still record many songs that they themselves have not written, although now the balance is shifting toward performers using their own material.

This discussion of how the music publishing business has evolved resonates through the rest of this book. While the roles of writers and publishers have changed, the structure of the business as it was originally created still remains. To wit, the concept of splitting writer and publisher income on a 50/50 basis still exists in almost every area of the music publishing business. Even if you, Joe Schmoe, wrote a song and started your own music publishing company, Schmoe Songs, there is still the traditional splitting of income. ASCAP or BMI will pay half of the public performance income earned by your song to Joe Schmoe (the writer) and the remaining half to Schmoe Songs (the publisher). You are still receiving 100% of the income, but you are receiving it in two different pockets (two payments on two statements). This convention of a *writer half* and a *publisher half* persists and contributes to difficulty and confusion relevant to the collection, licensing, and allocation of royalties. Actually, if it weren't for such atavistic conventions, music publishing would be a lot less complicated and require less math and logic, and songwriters could do a lot more for themselves.

The intricacies and finer points of writer shares, publisher shares, and splits will be further explained in later chapters. The appendix lays out some mathematical examples as well.

Digging Deeper

If you have absorbed the information in this chapter alone, you already know more about music publishing than many (most?) of the people you will deal with in the music business. The remaining chapters go into greater depth on many of the topics touched upon here (as well as others) and can be used for additional learning, research, or reinforcement.

The Value of Music

Dedicated to Martin Cohen, who wasn't afraid to walk away from a deal if the money wasn't right.

This chapter is written as a subjective defense against those who devalue or undervalue music. Just as those who overvalue and overprice music have damaged the legitimate consumption of music and instead encouraged rampant theft, so too have some people in the music world damaged their own product by undervaluing and underpricing it.

Music is a unique commodity with the ability to touch the soul or evoke an emotion or feeling. In a film, it might take minutes of dialogue or visual exposition to create a mood or tell a story, while music can instantly convey a mood or direction and give cues to the director's vision. Try imagining *Apocalypse Now* without the Doors' "The End" or without "Ride of the Valkyries," or *Casablanca* without "As Time Goes By." Typically, a feature film has at least 40 minutes of musical scoring. When was the last time you saw a film that had no musical score?

Likewise, some sports—figure skating, for instance—would not be possible without music. Imagine a college football game without a marching band. Restaurants and stores set the ambiance for you by playing background music.

Yet in the music publishing industry, no day goes by without someone who recognizes the value that music brings to a project nonetheless belittles its value, complains about its cost, and tries to pay less than a fair fee. It is important that writers and publishers stand tall and recognize and respect the value of their own property.

If they themselves fail to recognize the worth of their product, how can others be expected to see its worth and pay a reasonable price for it?

Many creators of music are today being marginalized. The media is full of articles about "file sharing" and how it hurts the music industry. What a nice euphemism, file sharing! Sharing is good, right? We are taught to share from the time we are little. But why does the media not do stories about the theft of intellectual property or copyright infringement? "File sharing" sounds so much more innocuous than "willful copyright infringement," which, by the way, is a felony. If I steal your car, is that "ride sharing?" By spinning articles and headlines in this manner, the media devalues the songs and artists.

More and more people who used to just get by on low-budget music careers, maybe by playing a few sessions, putting out self-released CDs, and doing a two-month tour of small clubs or coffeehouses, are no longer able to do so. There are many who must now work in fast-food restaurants and other low-paying jobs. It's getting harder to eke out an existence and to buy time to develop one's musical craft. This is not a simple problem, with only one cause and one solution. While piracy and copyright theft each play an important role in this phenomenon, and while overpricing makes theft feel more justifiable, writers and publishers who lack enough self-respect to value their songs appropriately contribute to the problem.

"This Is a Low-Budget Production"

Almost every license request a music publisher receives includes somewhere in it the words "This is a low-budget [film/TV show/record/ad campaign blah blah blah]." No one ever sends license requests that start off like, "This is a big-budget film, with two stars who are each getting 20 million dollars and a director who won the Academy Award for Best Picture last year. We would like to use the 'cherry' of your catalog and pay you a really nice fee for doing so." Or like this: "We have a multinational client who burned down half the Amazon rain forest last year and sold 300 million hamburgers and made 10 billion dollars in profit, and we would like to pay you some very significant money to join us in our destruction of the planet." It just doesn't happen.

Why is the same company that is paying 2 million dollars for the network broadcast time of its Superbowl spot balking at paying $250,000 to use your song for an entire year, and not just on the Superbowl? Budgets are low because people set them low. If there is no money in the music budget of a TV show, it is because the money they put into catering and hairdressing and makeup artists dwarfs the money allocated for music. Don't stand for it!

If you tried the same tactics in real life that are used in licensing music, you'd be laughed at. If you went into a Bentley dealership and said, "Gee, I sure like that $375,000 Azure, but I only have $30,000 to spend on a car, so do you think you could accept that?" you'd be shown the door along with some shoe leather. The idea that music has no intrinsic value leads to the proposal that "you should price your product according to our budget." Don't do it— especially if the song being inquired after is a standard, was a major hit, or has a lyrical or other connotation that is truly special. The situation may be different, though, if someone is inquiring about a generic punk song and the artist and song could be easily interchanged with many others.

"It Will Be Good Exposure"

Once they get done telling you how low they've set their budget and how you have to conform to what they've predetermined, they will pull out the old "good exposure" argument. While the licensers themselves are only working for real dollars and maybe profit participation, they would like you to please take your compensation in the form of good exposure.

Vaudeville entertainer Sophie Tucker, so the story goes, was once offered a gig at far less than her normal fee. The reason she should do it, the argument went, was that it would be good exposure. "Exposure?" she is said to have replied. "Isn't that what you die from?"

The worst cases of "licensing by exposure" lately seem to be in the realm of video-game music licensing. With some of the "shoot the whore"–type video games now selling for $30 a pop and shipping 4 or 5 million units, you'd think they'd be able to spare more than $5,000 as a flat fee to license a song. Let's do some made-up math. Let's see, that's around $150 million in gross over-the-counter revenue, and maybe half filters back to the game developer. And paying $5,000 for each of 50 songs would be $250,000. And double that fee to clear the master recordings, so we're up to $500,000 out of the $75 million. Why not at least pay a royalty instead of a flat fee?

In the early days of video-game licensing it was typical to get a flat fee of $20,000 per song, and sometimes as much as $50,000 or more. Now, many of today's top young bands have bought into the good-exposure theory and license top nationally known songs for $2,000 to $5,000. Yet, as publishers, we don't see the results that all this good exposure will bring. We don't see a sudden surge (or even any surge, for that matter) when a hot new extreme sport game ships 2 million copies with your song blaring throughout various levels of the game and on the TV advertisements for it. It would be great to see some scientifically documented correlation between appearing in a video game and record sales, band awareness, tour ticket sales, or even public goodwill.

Another example of licensing by exposure has entered the TV world lately in the form of *ad cards*. The deal goes like this: If you let your song be used for a pittance, we will give you a two-second ad card at the end of the show stating, "Joe Schmoe's new record *Sing-along with Schmoe* is available on Schmoe-Tone Records at stores everywhere." Again, for these ad cards, it would be nice see some correlation or documentable benefits attained by foregoing a fair license fee.

A Foreign Idea

One approach to valuing music is more common overseas than in the United States. That approach, used primarily in advertising at this point, is to assign a percent value to the music in a given campaign. Typically, this value is based on about 5% of the total cost of the advertising campaign. This 5% pool is then allocated to all the music being used in the project. If a $10 million European advertising campaign embodies your song, a $500,000 music licensing fee (half each to the publisher and master owner) would fall within current norms.

Such an approach is admirable in that it takes a bigger-picture look at the value of music, but it can skew unreasonably when the project it is being applied to has either a very big or very small total cost. In those instances, subjective minimums and maximums within current norms should be applied.

Perhaps the reason that this approach is more common outside of the United States is that mechanical royalties in most countries are not based on *penny rates* (e.g., 8.5¢ per copy) but on percentages. For example, it would be typical that 8.3% of the dealer selling cost of a CD in a given territory might form an aggregate *mechanical royalty pool* according to local law or custom, and that pool is then allocated according to each publishers' number of songs or prorated aggregate playing time.

In any event, the percentage approach provides a good alternative perspective as to what is fair and how music fits into a whole project.

Step This Way

Another approach to valuing a music license (usually involving motion pictures) is with what is called a *step deal*. Typically, an up-front flat fee is paid for a use. Then, if the film does well at the box office or in home video sales, there are *bumps*, or performance rewards. For example, a license might provide $5,000 up front, and then if/when a film hits milestones of $5 million, $10 million, and $15 million, and $20 million, the producer pays the music publisher an additional $5,000 for each respective box office level.

The nice thing about this approach is that the producer is acknowledging the worth of the music, and even if he can't or won't pay you what it is worth now, he is willing to pay you a fair value, and maybe then some, if he has a success. The bad thing about this approach is that too many step deals can overexpose a song for little or no money, and drive a paying user away from a song that has too much low-budget exposure and association.

Subjective Tense

You might conclude at this juncture that the pricing of music licenses is a difficult, subjective decision. Music is a unique commodity, and it has high intrinsic value that should not be discounted by either creators or licensers. There are many ways of looking at the value of music, and also many people who would like to pay you less than what it is worth on any reasonable scale.

Publishers and songwriters must both internalize and publicly exude the conviction that what they possess is valuable. Through education and through discussions with experienced industry professionals, fair win-win license fees can be determined.

It is often prudent, too, for songwriters and individually owned publishing companies not to handle their own negotiations. It is much harder to play poker and make the right decisions if your own money is on the table. If you are playing with your own money, you are more emotionally involved and less able to make the best-odds decision. Your representative will be able to take a more levelheaded approach.

Inevitably, and by definition, maintaining a license value results in fewer licenses. But doing so ensures that others know you attach an intrinsic value to a work. You might lose a certain percentage of the low-cost opportunities that are presented, but obtaining fair and reasonable quotes for the ones that do come to fruition will more than pay for the ones lost, and ensure the long-term value of a given song.

An example of this scenario is played out frequently by a music publisher who owns a very well-known song with a catch phrase that easily lends itself to advertising. In connection with the song, the publisher is approached for advertising campaigns every year or two. The publisher has priced the advertising use of the song in a one-year U.S. TV campaign at $500,000. When the publisher is offered $75,000, he declines it. While some may look at this as $75,000 foregone, he looks at it as $425,000 gained. For if the publisher had approved the $75,000 use, no other firm would want to run advertisements during that same time period with that same song. His experience has taught him that $500,000 is what advertisers are willing to pay for his song, and his experience has convinced him that there will be a significant use request every couple of years.

Unfortunately, some potential users will not be willing or able to pay a fair fee. But for the long-term health of the music, it is important not to devalue the song by licensing it for whatever a user offers. Bentley would go out of business if its dealers negotiated car sales that way, and so will you.

Types of Publishing Deals

There are many types of publishing deals. The most important variables in the various deals are ownership, administration, the period of time, and financial or "banking" considerations. The typical names given to different types of publishing agreements are determined by these variables.

Ownership vs. Administration

For our discussion, it is especially important to understand the difference between *ownership* and *administration*. A clear distinction can be made by analogy. Let's consider an apartment building called the Smedley Arms, located in beautiful downtown Douglasville. The owner of Smedley Arms is Adolph Smedley, who lives in Cannes, France. Locally, he has hired Simon Snott to manage the Smedley Arms.

Snott takes vacancy applications, screens potential residents, collects rent, chases down deadbeat tenants for back rent, pays taxes, does minor repairs, calls contractors for major repairs, pays the mortgage and insurance on the building, and generally oversees the property for Adolph Smedley. Smedley pays Snott 5% of the collected rents less monthly costs. At the end of the month, Snott balances the checkbook, prepares a statement, and sends the remaining profit to Smedley in the south of France.

In this example, Smedley is the owner and Snott is the administrator. Smedley has the ultimate responsibility for and ownership of the building, but Snott runs the enterprise on a day-to-day basis. Smedley has complete ownership of the property (maybe subject to a bank mortgage) while Snott has no equity whatsoever in the property.

If Snott is good building manager, or administrator, then Smedley gets good and accurate accountings, prompt rent collections, careful attention to monthly costs, good long-term care, and care-free enjoyment of his property from half the world away. On the other hand, if Snott is an inattentive laggard, all sorts of things can go wrong. For example, if he does not paint over graffiti on the garage, the building will not look nice, and potential tenants will not want to rent the vacant units. If he does not take care of the cockroach infestation, other tenants will move out. And if Snott is a chain-smoking drunkard who watches soap operas all day long and forgets to keep track of who has paid the rent and who hasn't, Smedley will suffer. The same is true for publishing administration.

So now let's say Smedley realizes that his building is going to hell and flies back to Douglasville, only to find Snott passed out in a pool of his own vomit, running the building as a flophouse for transients. He immediately fires Snott, then personally restores the building to its prior state and starts interviewing new managers (administrators) so that he can return to his idle life in Cannes. He finally settles on Miss Lilly Logic, who has demanded and will receive 7.5% of the collected rents less monthly costs but is painstakingly reliable, with anal attention to detail. Smedley is obviously better off with Miss Lilly than with Simon Snott even though she charges a 50% higher fee for the job. The qualitative and subjective aspects of her work make hiring her an easy and smart decision for Smedley given the Snott alternative.

So, too, is it with publishing administration. Simply comparing percentages and ignoring the qualitative aspects of the administrators can be costly. The collections received for two (nonsingle) songs on a given album administered by two separate administrators each receiving a 10% administration fee will rarely be the same or even close. The income streams are almost always significantly different depending on the quality of the administration. Qualitative aspects include speed and accuracy of registrations and licensing, attention to detail, and persistence in following through.

Work for Hire

As discussed in the "More On Copyright" chapter, the most severe type of publishing deal is the work for hire. In a *work-for-hire* situation, you give up complete ownership and all administration rights for the life of the copyright. Legally speaking, too, you are not even recognized as the author or creator of the work. Compensation may be on a flat-fee basis, or the *employer for hire* may agree to pay you a portion or share of the proceeds.

Work-for-hire agreements are most common in film and television composing, where the studio wants to own and control the whole collaborative result and not have to keep checking with the owners of the incorporated elements. These agreements are also common in the advertising world for the creation of commercial jingles.

Typically, work-for-hire deals are for one-off projects and have finite creation requirements.

Songwriting

A *songwriting deal* usually refers to an arrangement whereby you agree to write a certain number of songs for someone else. The distinguishing feature here is that someone else will own and administer your songs, usually for the life of the copyrights. You are induced to enter into this type of deal usually by a regular salary, payment, royalties, or advance against future royalties.

Songwriting deals are becoming more and more rare, but they still exist in certain areas of the music business. They are the nine-to-five jobs of the songwriting industry.

Administration

An *administration deal* offers more flexibility for the writer and the publisher. Ownership is retained by the writer or his designated publisher. The day-to-day handling of the music copyrights is the job of an administrator that the publisher has hired. Because of typical restrictions in an administration deal as to what the administrator can or cannot do without explicit approval from the owner, it provides ultimate control without myriad responsibilities. Typical administration fees are in the 10%–15% range, but as noted above, the qualitative aspects of administration are quite important, and administrators cannot be compared just on a fee or percentage basis. (Remember our friends Smedley, Snott, and Logic?) Administration deals do not typically involve advanced royalties or guaranteed payments.

Another advantage to an administration deal is that the period of time is variable and short when compared to life-of-copyright deals (work-for-hire and songwriting deals, for example). Typically, administration deals are two or three years in length. So if you end up hiring a Snott, your copyrights are not destined to be mishandled forever. You can simply take your catalog away from one administrator and hire another at the end of the term.

Copublishing

A *copublishing deal* is a hybrid between a traditional songwriting agreement and something more akin to a simple administration deal. In a copublishing deal, ownership is traditionally (but not necessarily) shared on a 50%/50% basis. Administration is typically handled by the company to which you sell half of your song, on behalf of both the company's 50% interest and your 50% interest. The deals generally provide for ownership to continue for life of copyright, although in some instances there may be a reversion of sorts, allowing the original publisher (writer) to recover the assigned 50% interests in the copyrights or perhaps the administration rights to the 50% retained by the original writer/publisher after a period of time.

Because a transfer of both ownership and administration is involved, publishing companies are often willing to pay significant advances and guarantees as inducements for copublishing deals. Not only do these companies acquire the right to make money by providing administration services, but they also acquire some ownership equity in the asset itself, the song. They become both a Snott and half of a Smedley.

It is not hard for publishing companies to analyze and minimize the risk involved in offering copublishing deals. For example, a company offering a copublishing deal might investigate and determine that your first forthcoming CD has 12 songs on it that will each be paid at 8.5¢ each ($1.02 total), and that the record company will initially ship 75,000 copies backed by a $500,000 ad campaign, great press, and a video that is already airing on MTV four times a day. So if things proceed the way it looks like they will, your songs will likely earn $76,500 in mechanical royalties in just the few months after release.

If you are a new artist and a publisher offers you a $100,000 advance for a copublishing deal, this might seem like a huge amount of money, allowing you to buy your first car and put a down payment on a starter house. But remember that in this scenario, you have given away half the ownership of your copyrights and likely all of the administration rights for a long period of time, while the publishing company is essentially risking only the difference between the *recoupable* $100,000 it is giving you and the $76,500 that you will predictably earn, or $23,500. So the company has risked only $23,500 to acquire half of your copyrights on this album and possibly future albums for which you write the songs.

Much will be made of the 75%/25% split to make a proposed deal seem more in your favor than in the favor of the publishing company to whom you have sold half of your songs. A copublishing deal does not obviate the need of the publishers to pay royalties to a songwriter under the traditional writer-half/publisher-half arrangement discussed in the "Overview" chapter. Therefore, a songwriter making a copublishing agreement can expect to have his account credited for 75% of the nonperformance income received by the company he has made the copublishing deal with (i.e., 100% of the writer's half plus 50% of the publisher's half, or 75% of the total). For performance income received by the company he has made the copublishing deal with, the split will be 50%/50%, or half of the publisher's share of the performance income. (Remember that you as the writer will receive the writer's half of performance income directly from your own performing right society.)

Even if the numbers offered get bigger than our hypothetical $100,000 offer, there are some other important considerations to be given to a copublishing agreement. First, remember that the companies that are offering you the money are professional music-business bettors or handicappers of talent. If they consistently made back less in earnings than they handed out in advances, they would go out of business. So you may in fact be betting that you will earn less than these companies, which have a lot more experience in these matters than you do, think you will earn. In other words, you're betting against yourself with a professional bettor (that multinational music publishing company). Not only are these companies handicapping the likely success of your music, but they are covering their own overhead, the actual administration for your songs, the costs of advancing you the money, and their losses on writers who didn't make their money back for them.

Remember, too, that the money you are getting, while it might seem like a lot to write home about (trying to justify your meager existence to your folks who think that it is still not too late to give up your music career and become a doctor), might be less than it appears. If you get $250,000, you might pay 15% to a manager, 5% to an accountant or business manager, and $20,000 to the lawyer for making the deal, leaving you with $181,875. Except that you will be paying half in taxes, leaving you with a net $90,937.50. This amount may or may not justify giving up half your ownership and all your control (administration) for a long period of time.

Lastly, remember that you have no control over the quality of the administration and that who collects it and how they do it will no longer be your ultimate decision.

Copublishing deals offer short-term bird-in-the-hand money to writers, and they are also very popular with managers because they get an immediate payoff without having to wait for your career to actually develop and without actually having to work your record. If you're a flop, at least both of you got something up front. These deals effectively take some of your chips off of the table, cash you out, get you a partner, and spread the risk around. But they also hugely limit your upside and stick you into a long-term arrangement where you will have little or no direct control of your own work and have given up half of your ownership.

Once in a while, if you're very lucky, the hype about you and your songwriting might be so great, and the money offered might be so emotionally out of proportion with reality, as to seem laughable. The music business occasionally sees ferocious bidding wars between corporate lemmings all convinced that their prognosis of your success is rational because all their competitive counterparts envision it too. When the money gets bid up into the "stupid" stratosphere, this is probably the best time to seriously consider these offers, although just where the stupid stratosphere begins is unfortunately subjective. Noncommissioned and nonpaid advisors are useful in helping you balance your excitement, impatience, desperation, and genuine needs against what you might be giving up.

There are other cases, too, when knowingly taking a sure thing (the money in a copublishing deal) as opposed to maintaining the future upside (holding onto your full copyrights) simply provides piece of mind, stability, or meets pressing financial needs. These bird-in-the-hand situations should be carefully considered.

The Final Solution

Inevitably, there comes a time when songwriters, publishers, or heirs consider selling their songs (their *catalog*). To continue our apartment building analogy, song catalogs are sold in a very similar manner as investment real estate.

Apartment buildings are usually sold on the basis of the net amount of money they earn, or "throw off," per year. So too are publishing catalogs. Typically, a calculation is made of *net publisher's share*, or NPS. NPS is just like what it sounds like. It is the net amount that the publisher retains after paying writers, copublishers, administrators, and costs.

Buyers and sellers of catalogs typically remove any extraordinary or not-likely-to-be-repeated activity from NPS. Examples of this might be if there was a sudden spike or nonrepeatable increase in income for a few months due to a writer's death, or if the song becomes the official Superbowl theme in a given year. The nonextraordinary NPS for the last three (or possibly five) years is then averaged out. Sometimes an upward or downward trend is visible, but for most older catalogs, NPS will be more or less constant.

The average NPS is then multiplied by a mutually determined amount to arrive at a catalog sales price. Typical sales multiples are anywhere from 8 to 20, depending on the prestige of the catalog, income trending, exploitation possibilities, and the situations of the buyers and sellers. Most catalogs change hands now for 12 to 16 times NPS. So a catalog with a three-year annual average NPS of $100,000 per year might sell for $1.2 to $1.6 million.

A buyer can also analyze the expected rate of return by inverting the sales multiple. For example, a catalog that sells for a 12 times multiple has an annual rate of return to the buyer of 1/12th, or an 8.33% return on the investment. A catalog sale with an 8 times sales multiple represents a 1/8th annual return on investment, or 12.5%, while one with a 20 times sales multiple has a 5% return.

In valuing a catalog, care should also be taken to determine if and when the songs might be recoverable as discussed in the chapter "More On Copyright." If you are buying a catalog that only has three years left on the songs before the original writers are legally eligible to recover the songs, you would certainly want to heavily discount what you might be willing to pay. Correspondingly, if you are selling a catalog, you also want to take this factor into account in your pricing.

Don't forget that even if you are selling ownership to the copyrights, you still have the right to collect the writer royalties under the underlying agreements. If there are no underlying agreements, care should be taken to ensure the catalog sales agreement specifies that writer royalties are payable to the writers or heirs. Because NPS is calculated net of writers' royalties, the expectation of buyers is that they will still have to pay the writer's half to the writer or the writer's heirs. So even if you sell Dad's musical gems to some big corporation for millions of dollars, you still will have an ongoing income stream from the big corporation paying you Dad's writer royalties, but it will just be half of what it used to be. It is possible, too, to sell the writer's share to someone, but because writer's share is more like passive income and has no corresponding administration rights or control, it is more like buying or selling a passive annuity, and prices may be slightly discounted.

A great deal of caution should be taken in considering the sale of musical copyrights, and advice should be taken from someone quite knowledgeable in the field. Historically, musical copyrights throw off lots of money with little additional overhead. Income from musical copyrights, especially standards (songs that are recorded and licensed again and again), often rises, and thus so does the multiple value of NPS. Over the past 100 years, the value of significant music copyrights and the income they have produced make them among the best and steadiest investments one could have had. Their disposition should not be considered lightly. (Of course, this could all go to hell in a handbasket if people continue to steal music over the Internet and otherwise and the value of music and copyright becomes further eroded.)

Beware the Jabberwock, My Son

While we have talked about the importance of the qualitative aspects of publishing administration, it is equally important to disregard (or at least take with a big grain of salt) the intangible promises that will be made to you to get your signature on the dotted line. At some point in the process of trying to sign you to a publishing deal, most companies will trot out an extra-friendly person to love-bomb you and sell you on a fantastic vision of what they can and will do for you. No doubt, this person (the *professional manager*) will know every music supervisor in Hollywood, will tell you about all the songs that he or she has recently gotten into which film/commercial/CD, and is close personal friends with Producer X who is looking for songs for Superstar Y's new album.

In the vast majority of instances, you will be shocked and awed into believing that this person *loves* your songs and *really* has the connections to do something for you. Be cynical here. I certainly am. Most big breaks happen organically and are not forced or suggested by a professional manager. If your songs are registered properly with ASCAP, BMI, or SESAC, people will be able to contact you when they want to license your songs. Professional managers, in my opinion, are mostly there to field these calls that would come in anyway, though they try to give you the impression that they have generated the interest.

If this kind of professional activity worked as well as the managers would have you believe it does, then "professional" departments would be the largest departments at any publishing company. They are not. It is very, very hard to find and hire professional managers who are truly able to generate enough new activity for a song or catalog that they not only earn back their own salary but make significant money for the company they work for. These genuinely effective people are extraordinarily rare in the music business. But pretend effective people are useful as window dressing to get you to believe that they will really do something for you if you sign up.

Song Plugging

These people who promise to open doors for you sometimes make deals directly with songwriters and publishers that only have straight administration deals. They are known as *song pluggers*, and they offer to put their active and professional magic to work for you. Hiring one of these people to work on your behalf may be worthwhile, but with a few provisos.

First, the work that they do should be compensated by results they obtain. They should not get a fee, administration rights, or any copyright co-ownership for what they promise they will do. Any compensation or benefits they receive from you should be solely as reward for results they actually deliver.

A song plugger should not have the right to bind you to a deal or commit your song to a use without your approval. Many of the leads and offers that a typical song plugger turns up are of limited or dubious value. It is easy to find low-budget film and television producers who are just begging to find cheap music to fill their project while promising great exposure. A song plugger who wants a piece of your copyright because he got you a $500 film synchronization fee, which you only accepted because you didn't want to dampen his enthusiasm, will not be of any great benefit to you or your songs.

Where possible, it is far better to compensate song pluggers with a share of the income as opposed to a share of the ownership (equity) in your copyright. Pay rent; don't give away the building.

The best song pluggers are aggressive writers and publishers who actively network on their own behalf. The best song plugger I know is one of the most successful songwriters of the 20th century. Not a day goes by when she isn't calling a producer in the studio, having lunch with an A&R man, or calling a record company head. Even for those who don't have this kind of high-level access, there is always someplace to start with polite and gentle networking—a bar where musicians hang out, recording studios and sessions, music seminars and meetings such as those sponsored by ASCAP or BMI, friends, or organizations like the Association of Independent Music Publishers, the National Music Publishers Association, or the California Copyright Conference.

Big-name artists and writers get writer's block all the time, and you'd be surprised how many would just love to coast on one of your great musical ideas. Approaching them with, "Hey, I've written a great chorus but I can't seem to finish the verses—can you take a listen and see if you could finish it up?" may be quite intriguing. Even if it is not and the door gets slammed in your face, the most successful pluggers, like the most successful salesmen, don't take it personally and simply go on to the next door. You are your own best champion.

No Deal At All

Another possibility is to make no publishing deal at all and do everything yourself. This can be done but requires a lot of self-educating. A reasonably intelligent person is certainly capable of figuring out how to correctly complete the appropriate copyright form. It also isn't that hard to join ASCAP, BMI, or SESAC as both a writer and a publisher, and to register your songs. While paying close attention to the points raised in the mechanical licensing chapter, it is possible to issue your own mechanical licenses and not screw up too badly.

If you're self-administering your songs and, say, had a CD that only came out in Japan, you could probably do some research, find a good Japanese subpublisher, and make a three-year subpublishing deal. But if the record comes out worldwide and you need to make and handle 15 or 20 subpublishing deals, you just might find yourself in the publishing business instead of the songwriting business.

I urge songwriters to try to do some of these things by themselves, or with the help of knowledgeable people, because the education, understanding, and frame of reference that you will derive from the process will be valuable once you get to the point of choosing between being a full-time publishing administrator or being a full-time songwriter.

I Have It Here Someplace

Whatever type of publishing deal you make, make sure you keep a fully executed copy of the final deal in a safe place where you will never lose it. You should have in your own possession final copies of all the contracts and documents you ever sign. The tendency is to rely on lawyers, managers, or others to maintain these documents for you, but taking this one simple step will save you more time, money, and aggravation than you could ever conceive.

Mechanical Licenses

Let's talk more about mechanical licenses and uses. If you did not read the "Overview" chapter and clearly comprehend what a mechanical license and royalty is, and how it differs from an artist royalty, you shouldn't be reading this chapter yet. If necessary, review the earlier material and then come back here when you're ready to absorb more detail.

Mechanical licenses cover many types of devices that can be used to reproduce music. Without limitation, a mechanical license can cover vinyl records, cassette tapes, eight-track tapes, DAT tapes, CDs, DVD-As, music files such as MP3 recordings permanently delivered via the Internet, and even piano rolls and music boxes. These formats are generally lumped together under the name *phonorecords*, which in copyright law are defined as "material objects in which sounds, other than those accompanying a motion picture or other audiovisual work, are fixed by any method now known or later developed, and from which the sounds can be perceived, reproduced, or otherwise communicated, either directly or with the aid of a machine or device."

Hybrid formats that contain visual synchronizations or lyrics, however, do not constitute mechanical uses. For example, a karaoke disc that embodies visual images and has lyrics shown on a screen from which they may be read does not constitute a mechanical use.

Likewise, a DVD of a movie that features music as part of soundtrack constitutes a synchronization and not a mechanical use. While such a use is referred to as a *video mechanical*, it has different legal properties and the publisher is under no obligation to grant such a license. A mechanical use must involve audio-only reproductions of music.

Compulsory Licenses

The most basic type of mechanical license is called a *compulsory license*. A compulsory license allows anyone to manufacture and distribute phonorecords of nondramatic musical works to the general public. There are several requirements that must be followed by the user. Of greatest importance, the musical work in question must have already been publicly distributed in the United States with the copyright owner's (music publisher's) consent. Once you have authorized public distribution of your song for the first time, anyone who wants to release and distribute your song may do so *without your approval*, provided he/she follows the compulsory license provisions of copyright law.

Let's look at this a little closer. Say you have written a song on the piano for your sister to tell her how much you love her. The only ones who have heard this are you and your sister. Can Michael Jackson, recognizing that you have written a sure-fire hit, get a compulsory license and release a record of your song? No! But what if you and your sister love Michael Jackson's song "Beat It," which *was* commercially released and publicly distributed on Michael Jackson's *Thriller* album? Even though the two of you can't sing worth beans, and even though you want to do a heavy metal goth reggae version of the song and release it for public sale on your website and in stores, you can go right ahead! Provided that you don't change "the basic melody or fundamental character of the work," and that you are not adding new copyrightable material of your own (such as extra verses or different musical interludes), you only have to follow the compulsory license provisions of the copyright law in order to share your take on "Beat It" with the world.

Compulsory License Requirements

So what are these compulsory license provisions that you have to follow so as not to run afoul of Mr. Jackson and his attorneys, who so detest heavy metal goth reggae music? Well, §201.18 through §201.20 of the U.S. copyright law tell you what to do. But rather than reproduce that spine-tingling prose here, I will summarize it. Of course, this is just an overview of what is involved, and you should really go to the actual law if you want to make sure you're in full compliance. (The U.S. Copyright Office makes a lot of law and summarizing pamphlets that it calls *circulars* available online at www.copyright.gov.)

First, you have to find the copyright owner (the music publisher) of the song. You can check with the Copyright Office to do this, and there are provisions to follow that will allow you to proceed even if you can't find the copyright owner. Next, you have to serve the owner/publisher with a "Notice of Intention to Obtain a Compulsory License" (your friends at the Copyright Office can tell you how to do this) by certified or registered mail, and you have to do this prior to or on the 30th day of your intended release. Of course, being a cheapskate, you will send this notice by certified mail since it is so much cheaper than registered mail.

Finally, you have to pay Mr. Jackson's publisher the full statutory royalty rate. Currently, that rate is 8.5¢ for a recording under five minutes in length. Unfortunately, you and your sister made an excruciating recording that lasts for 9:12. So you have to pay the so-called *long-song* rate, which is currently 1.65¢ per minute or fraction thereof. (A nifty chart with the U.S. mechanical rates from 1909 through at least January 1, 2006, is reproduced on the following page.) Since you have 9 minutes and one fraction thereof (the 12 seconds), you have to pay Mr. Jackson's publisher ten times 1.65¢, or 16.5¢, per copy you make and distribute of your wretched record. Hell, he should be paying you not to put it out!

The way that you have to account and pay to Mr. Jackson's publisher is, relatively speaking, onerous and difficult. Among other requirements, the compulsory license statements must be rendered on a monthly basis, and they must be signed and certified as truthful and accurate in very specific ways. There are also lots of other obnoxious hoops you have to jump through, so basically, no one really does mechanical licensing this way unless there's no alternative.

United States Mechanical Rates

Date	Rate	Authority
1909–1977	2 cents per minute of playing time or fraction thereof, whichever is greater	Copyright Act of 1909
January 1, 1978	2 3/4 cents or .5 cent	Copyright Act of 1976
January 1, 1981	4 cents or .75 cent per minute of playing time or fraction thereof, whichever is greater	1980 Mechanical Rate Adjustment Proceeding
January 1, 1983	4.25 cents or .8 cent per minute of playing time or fraction thereof, whichever is greater	1980 Mechanical Rate Adjustment Proceeding
July 1, 1984	4.5 cents or 8.5 cent per minute of playing time or fraction thereof, whichever is greater	1980 Mechanical Rate Adjustment Proceeding
January 1, 1986	5 cents or .95 cent per minute of playing time or fraction thereof, whichever is greater	1980 Mechanical Rate Adjustment Proceeding
January 1, 1988	5.25 cents or 1 cent per minute of playing time or fraction thereof, whichever is greater	1980 Mechanical Rate Adjustment Proceeding
January 1, 1990	5.7 cents or 1.1 cent per minute of playing time or fraction thereof, whichever is greater	1980 Mechanical Rate Adjustment Proceeding
January 1, 1992	6.25 cents or 1.2 cent per minute of playing time or fraction thereof, whichever is greater	1980 Mechanical Rate Adjustment Proceeding
January 1, 1994	6.6 cents or 1.25 cent per minute of playing time or fraction thereof, whichever is greater	1980 Mechanical Rate Adjustment Proceeding
January 1, 1996	6.95 cents or 1.3 cents per minute of playing time or fraction thereof, whichever is greater	1980 Mechanical Rate Adjustment Proceeding
January 1, 1998	7.1 cents or 1.35 cents per minute of playing time or fraction thereof, whichever is greater	1980 Mechanical Rate Adjustment Proceeding
January 1, 2000	7.55 cents or 1.45 cents per minute of playing time or fraction thereof, whichever is greater	1980 Mechanical Rate Adjustment Proceeding
January 1, 2002	8.0 cents or 1.55 cents per minute of playing time or fraction thereof, whichever is greater	1980 Mechanical Rate Adjustment Proceeding
January 1, 2004	8.5 cents or 1.65 cents per minute of playing time or fraction thereof, whichever is greater	1980 Mechanical Rate Adjustment Proceeding
January 1, 2006	9.1 cents or 1.75 cents per minute of playing time or fraction thereof, whichever is greater	1980 Mechanical Rate Adjustment Proceeding

Mechanical Licenses in the Real World

In the real world, neither record companies nor publishers really want to deal with compulsory licenses. Record companies don't want to send publishers statements on a monthly basis, and, frankly speaking, most publishers don't want to get royalty statements to process every 30 days. On top of that, for reasons that you are free to guess, no one at any record company wants to hand-sign any statement that by law has to say "I certify that I have examined this Monthly Statement of Account and that all statements of fact contained herein are true, complete, and correct to the best of my knowledge, information, and belief, and are made in good faith."

So what to do? Well, the first step is still the same. You and your sister still have to find Mr. Jackson's publisher. But then, you *ask* them very nicely if you can please have a mechanical license. They could ask to listen to your and your sister's lousy version of "Beat It" and say, "Whoa, no, we're going to make you freaks go through compulsory license notices and provisions." Or they could say, "Hey, you're only making 100 copies of your CD, so it will cost us more to issue the license than the $16.50 we're going to be paid (100 copies times the 16.5¢ long-song rate), so you have to go through compulsory license notices and provisions."

However, in most cases, they will send you a license if you act professionally and provide them with a nice, neat (neatness counts) request telling them all the stuff they might want to know, such as: the name and address of your record label, the name of your group, the release date, the record number, phonorecord format(s) (e.g., CD, tape, etc.), and the running time of your recording. Such license, typically, will provide that you only need to account to them and pay them on a quarterly basis, usually within 45 days of quarter end. In fact, though, the "mechanical licenses" that publishers send out are, when read carefully, not actual licenses, but waivers of compulsory license provisions to which the publisher agrees.

Specifically, the "mechanical license" will usually say something to the effect that we are waiving the requirement that we receive a "Notice of Intention to Obtain a Compulsory License," and we are waiving the requirement that you account to us every 30 days, and we are waiving the requirement that you hand-sign that horrible statement whereby you promise to be truthful and honest, and all you have to do is pay us every quarter, and gosh darn it you better be honest about it.

You're a Publisher Again

The U.S. copyright law, as discussed above, is very detailed about the requirements on mechanical licensing and accounting. In many cases, especially where an independent publisher is involved, a record company will only be too happy to prepare and submit a mechanical license for a publisher to sign, granting the record company the right to mechanically reproduce your (the publishing company's) song. You don't want to do this.

A mechanical license is not a mechanical license is not a mechanical license. If you only have the little knowledge that amounts to a "dangerous thing," the record company will take advantage of you (surprising, isn't it?). Here are some things that labels may try to get for their own benefit.

- They would like it if your license is not specific to a given recording artist or record number. That way, whenever in the future they want to use your song, they will not have to ask for a license, since your license is a *blanket license* that gives that label the right to use your song on any product or with any recording artist without the necessity of checking with you.

- They would like it if your license specifies a penny rate (e.g., 8.5¢) as opposed to being listed as statutory, so the license is not subject to increases in the statutory rate in the future.

- Even if they do offer you a statutory rate, they may add several undesirable modifiers such as "minimum statutory rate" (which means that a long-song rate, where applicable, will not apply) or a "statutory rate as of the date hereof" (which means that even though they are paying you the statutory rate, it is fixed in time at "the date hereof" and is not subject to any future increase in that rate).

- They would like to pay you on the basis of records "manufactured and sold" or "manufactured, sold, and not returned" as opposed to what the Copyright Office and compulsory license provisions require of them as an accounting basis, which is "manufactured and distributed" (note that distributed records are not necessarily sold).

- They would like to have rate reductions for phonorecords sold/distributed at mid-line or budget price points, or through record clubs, and they'd even like the rate waived for records they give away for free. (*Free goods* are, in record industry terminology, *not* records given away for promotional value. They are *bonus records* that are given to the stores for free with each paid order. The stores then *sell* the "free goods" to the general public. A typical record company "free goods" program might give the store an incentive along the lines that it pays for 85 CDs and gets an extra 15 CDs for free that it can also sell. In the absence of a good reason, music publishers should be—and frequently are—paid on all or some of the free goods. *Promotional records* such as those given to reviewers, journalists, and radio stations are, if within a reasonable number or percentage of total sales, typically exempted from payment of mechanical royalties because of music publishers' good nature. This need not be the case, though, due to the "manufactured and distributed" copyright law requirement.)

- They would like to pay you every six months instead of quarterly (or even monthly), and would like to pay you 60 or 90 days after the period end instead of the normal 45 days.

- They would like pay you for only on one "use" per record. But what if your song is reprised? Or what if a CD contains three different mixes of your song?

These are just *some* of the things you should look for. In short, mechanical licensing, while seemingly simple and straightforward, is fraught with difficulty and the potential for missteps. A music publisher should know what perils to avoid with mechanical licensing, because a simple, innocuous-looking one-page document can have serious deleterious long-term consequences.

In addition, there is one great weapon that record companies use to pay publishers less favorably than they would otherwise be entitled under the copyright law, and that is the *controlled composition clause*. These clauses are found in recording agreements and primarily affect recording artists who are also writers/publishers of their own material. The controlled composition clause, which will be discussed in greater detail in a later chapter, makes the recording artist guarantee that the record company will have many additional benefits with respect to mechanical (and even video) licensing. In some circumstances, legally speaking, a controlled composition clause can even be made to apply to music publishers and songwriters who are not subject to or signatories to the applicable recording agreement. (The reasons for this horrible "I didn't sign it and I'm still legally bound by it?" situation concern nonexclusive licenses issued by copublishers and are discussed in the chapter on cowriters and copublishers.)

Reduced Rate Licensing

It is very common for music publishers to be approached by potential users who want to release phonorecords and pay less than the statutory rate. Most common is the *three-quarter rate* request where a record company states its desire to obtain a mechanical license at a rate equal to 75% of the statutory rate. If you went to your local gas station and gas was $2 a gallon, you'd have to give the proprietors a pretty good reason to sell you a tankful at $1.50 a gallon. Perhaps if you offered to have them tune up your car or if you bought a set of tires, they would see enough overall profit and let you have the gasoline at that reduced price.

Other than via a controlled composition clause, where a pre-existing reduced mechanical rate agreement already exists, the music publisher is in charge of the situation and needs some pretty good reasons to offer a 25% discount on a product. The most typical incentive given is an advance.

The record company will offer you an advance, frequently on a number of units, if you discount the mechanical rate by 25%. For example, if you agree to a three-quarter rate (i.e., you get 6.38¢ per unit instead of 8.5¢ per unit for a use less than five minutes), the company will pay you up front for 25,000 units (6.38¢ times 25,000 = $1,593.75). The advantages are that you are getting your money for the first 25,000 units in advance, and that if the record doesn't sell 25,000 units, you're ahead of the game. On the other hand, you've just waived $531.25 in income, and if the record does sell more than 25,000 units, you're in for a permanent long-term discount.

Typical unit advance offers for reduced mechanical licenses are 25,000 units and up. I have seen offers for 100,000 units, 500,000 units, and more. Obviously, the higher the unit advance, the more tempting the proposition. Likewise, offers much below 25,000 units provide, relatively speaking, very little incentive. A 15,000-unit advance represents less than $1,000 for a permanent 25% reduction in your income. It gets even worse when a publisher controls only part of a song. If a publisher controls 25% of a song that has four writers, a three-quarter rate for 15,000 units means giving up 25% of the mechanical income for less than $250 up front.

By the way, there is no reason why reduced rate requests necessarily have to be on a 3/4 basis, and occasionally music publishers get 50% of statutory request or 87.5% of statutory, etc.

Another argument a record company will give for a reduced rate mechanical license is that it is a very small company and cannot afford a full rate. In other words, the company would like you to treat them charitably. Some publishers do, in fact, enjoy helping the little guy. Others find such requests disingenuous, as the smaller the company and the smaller the given release size, the less the difference in rate actually matters. If such record company is asking you to accept a 3/4 rate on a release with a 500-unit initial pressing, it is asking that instead of ultimately paying you $42.50 if all units manufactured are distributed, it will pay you $31.88, a savings to them of $10.63. In this case, the favor that you are doing for the little guy is so marginal, and the publisher's cost of interacting and/or preparing a license doesn't change.

This brings up what, in my office, is referred to as the Law of Inverse Effort. There seems to be a pattern that when you're dealing with large amounts of money and very significant licenses, the deals get done much more quickly and easily than when you're dealing with small amounts of money and insignificant licenses (our 500-unit friend, for example), which seem to take a lifetime to finalize. The theorized reason for this is that those empowered to handle the bigger licenses have more experience and know-how, and understand industry practice and norms, while those working on the tiny little deals may not know the first thing about what they are trying to do, and can and will waste a great deal of your time.

As a music publisher, you could find yourself very frustrated with the little-guy label, who then brings in his brother-in-law, the personal injury attorney, to help close the deal, only frustrating you more because the guy doesn't know anything about copyright law or mechanical licenses but thinks he can handle it just because he is an attorney! Although well intentioned, the proverbial favor to the little guy could be the nightmare that never goes away in terms of your time and effort. So if you're the little-guy record company, please bear this rant in mind and remember that professionalism can and will be rewarded.

So, after all that, why grant a reduced-rate mechanical license? Sometimes you just wanna play ball. Most of the major record labels (including Warner, Sony, BMG, Universal, and Capitol-EMI) have "special market" units that assemble and market compilation records (*Best of the '80s, Music for Lovers, Songs That Start with the Letter S*). If a publisher wants to have his music included on these various records, he may be inclined to participate in the reduced-rate racket. The thinking goes, "If I never approve the reduced-rate requests, they'll stop calling me and use some other publisher's songs on all their compilation albums. Especially since they don't need to use my song for this compilation and especially since there are lots of other songs that start with the letter *S*."

Another good reason to grant a reduced-rate mechanical license is if a song is a split copyright and your copublisher or cowriter asks you to. You might not want to hold out for a full rate when your equal writing partner is only getting 3/4 for his half. Getting 25% more than a partner gets for his equal share, or even worse, making the cowriter or copublisher pay the additional 25% to you out of his own pocket, is often awkward and thus a good reason to play along.

Reduced-rate licenses, finally, are frequently, but not always, granted on what is called a *most favored nations* basis, abbreviated as MFN. What that means is that the licenser is guaranteeing you the best deal that he is giving anyone. If he offers you a 75% rate on an MFN basis, and then later offers someone an 85% statutory rate, he will have to raise your rate to the "most favored" 85% rate. In this way, publishers tie their fate to other publishers and get a guarantee that they are getting the most favorable deal offered. A word of caution, too, is that the most favored nations provisions should apply to all material terms, not just mechanical licensing rates. Specifically, MFN terms should at least apply to both the amount or number of units of advance given and to the statutory rate of payment. You might not want to get a most favored nations advance and rate reduction when some people are foregoing the advance altogether and getting a full statutory rate.

It may be a justifiable policy, too, that with certain very important catalogs, writers, or songs, a music publisher will not under any circumstances grant a reduced-rate mechanical license. It all depends on what you're selling, and how valuable it is.

Harry Who?

In the United States there is a licensing organization known as the Harry Fox Agency. HFA is primarily known for issuing mechanical licenses (compulsory license provision waivers, as discussed above, actually). For a fee, Harry Fox will issue mechanical licenses on behalf of music publishers and perform associated and related services. (As of April 1, 2004, Harry Fox charges 6.75% of the mechanical income received plus an annual fee ranging from $200 to $800 per year depending on gross annual revenues.) Because

Harry Fox controls the United States mechanical licensing on a large percent of the domestic music publishing repertoire, the organization should be mentioned simply to acknowledge its existence. My experiences and interactions with the organization over more than 25 years have been very poor. Accordingly, I neither use HFA's services nor recommend its services to others.

There are other, smaller, lesser-known mechanical licensing firms operating in the United States as well. In my opinion, there is no better alternative to direct mechanical licensing and collection between qualified music publishers and publishing administrators and the end user of the mechanical license. Communication and collection are thus direct between two principals without a third-party intermediary.

Oh! Canada!

Mechanical licensing in Canada can also be handled effectively directly between U.S. publishers and Canadian record companies. Many of the basic points are similar. Here are the prevailing Canadian mechanical royalty rates, expressed in Canadian dollars (at this writing, $1 Canadian is equal to approximately $.76 U.S.).

Canadian Mechanical Rates (in Canadian Currency)

1988	5.25¢/1.05¢ per minute
1990	5.9¢/1.18¢ per minute
1992	6.25¢/1.25¢ per minute
1994	6.47¢/1.294¢ per minute
1996	6.6¢/1.32¢ per minute
1998	7.1¢/1.42¢ per minute
2000	7.4¢/1.48¢ per minute
2002	7.7¢/1.54¢ per minute

The Canadians, though, have done something interesting. They abolished the statutory mechanical rate in 1988. Music publishers are thus free to negotiate and charge whatever they want to charge a Canadian record company for mechanical reproduction. Why then, are standardized mechanical rates shown in the chart?

The reason is that there is a Canadian licensing organization analogous to the Harry Fox Agency called the CMRRA (Canadian Musical Reproduction Rights Agency). While I do not use the CMRRA for mechanical licensing, I do use and advocate its services for other types of Canadian licensing, specifically the Canadian Broadcast Mechanical Tariff (a mechanical-type fee charged to broadcasters for making duplicate copies of works) and the Canadian Blank Media Levy (a fee charged in Canada to manufacturers of blank media such as blank tapes and blank CD and DVD media under the assumption that at least some of the people buying this blank recording media are making copies of copyrighted material, and that there should therefore be a "tax" levied and paid to copyright proprietors such as music publishers). The CMRRA represents the majority of music publishers' songs in Canada, and on their behalf has negotiated mechanical licensing rates and terms with another Canadian organization, the CRIA (Canadian Recording Industry Association), which represents the vast majority of Canadian record companies.

At the date of writing, the most recent mechanical licensing rates negotiated by the CMRRA and CRIA, referred to as *schemes*, were agreed effective on January 1, 1998, for a period of six years (as of November 2004, the new rates had not yet been determined). The rates given in the chart are not binding upon non-CMRRA publishers or non-CRIA record companies, but these rates are "usual and customary" for the vast majority of music publishers and record companies and are used in almost all instances by companies not affiliated with either of those two trade organizations. But please remember, there is no *obligation* for a non-CMRRA publisher to accept these rates. The CMRRA-CRIA scheme also makes provisions for other sorts of rates, limits, and even makes provisions for ignoring certain artist-controlled composition provisions (see chapter on controlled composition clauses).

Armed with the foregoing knowledge, it is not difficult for a U.S. music publisher to issue mechanical licenses to a Canadian record company. Many of the Canadian record companies will even (upon request) convert the Canadian dollar earnings into U.S. dollars and pay you in preconverted funds. Due to NAFTA and other tax laws, there is generally no tax on Canadian royalties paid to a U.S. company.

Due to the Quebecois preference for French, Canadian record companies based in that province sometimes ask you to insert this or similar wording into a mechanical (or other) license agreement:

"The parties hereto hereby request that this license be drawn up in the English language. (Les parties aux présentes ont demandé que cette licence soit rédigée en langue anglais.)"

Go on, humor them. Canadians are nice people. Their country is a small but important music market. Canada has just over 10% of the U.S. population (32 million vs. 290 million), but its quality is high.

Record Clubs

There are currently two significant record clubs in the United States: the Columbia House Record Club and the BMG Record Club. They both have online versions and video clubs as well. The Columbia House Club also operates in Canada.

One of the original ideas behind the record clubs was to sell records through the mail in areas of the country not serviced by major chains. However, with the advent of the Internet, it is now possible for pretty much anyone anywhere to have access to overnight shipping for virtually any record currently available (and even out of print). The record clubs were also viewed and/or designed to obtain supplemental and incremental sales as opposed to displacing bricks-and-mortar record-store sales. Record stores were given an exclusive sales period before a record was available through a record club at a discounted price. Once all the customers interested in obtaining a new album soon after its release date had made their purchases (at full price), then it would become available to the people who had marginal interest in the product, either because of the price or because of a perceived difficulty in going to the store and buying it. Record clubs would induce such consumers to make purchases by offering home delivery, lower prices, and tempting commitment offers (Get 10 free CDs now! Pay only shipping! And you agree to buy three more at normal club prices during the next year!).

There is substantial debate in the music industry as to whether record-club sales represent supplemental marginalized purchases, or whether they are cannibalizing normal full-price consumer sales. Are people buying more and different records than they would have without the clubs, or are they waiting for particular CDs to hit the clubs and then buying them at reduced prices? One thing is for sure: recording artists get greatly reduced artist royalties for record-club sales and often do not get paid at all for vast numbers of membership-inducement units that the clubs give away.

So how do record clubs deal with music publishers' mechanical royalties? Put simply, the clubs take the position that they don't need to serve a Notice of Intention to Obtain a Compulsory License as required by U.S. copyright law. They say they don't have to obtain mechanical licenses or waivers of compulsory terms from music publishers. They further claim they have the right not to pay the full statutory mechanical royalty for each record they distribute and instead to pay only 75% of the normal statutory rate. The clubs take many other tenuous and provocative positions too with respect to songs with copublishers.

Is this legal? I do not believe so and attempted to litigate these issues against the clubs several years ago. The case was dismissed (wrongly in my opinion) on a Motion for Summary Judgment. For various reasons including potential financial liability for the clubs' legal and other costs in the event of an unsuccessful appeal, I elected not to pursue the case further or appeal the summary judgment decision.

Recently, however, I learned that Max Blecher and Neville Johnson, two attorneys well versed in both music business matters and class-action suits, have filed a complaint against the record clubs seeking judicial clarification and/or damages in the matters and positions discussed above affecting music publishers. The judge in the case recently certified the class status and stated that the "Wixen" case is an unpublished opinion that does not constitute law, and thus allowed the case to move forward.

Given large potential liability, the record clubs decided to settle the case, and under the proposed settlement will pay $6.5 million to the publishers and be required to obtain publisher approvals for reduced rate payments by posting on the Internet notices of intent to use. Final court approval on the settlement was expected in February 2005.

Those Other Foreigners

How are mechanical royalties handled outside of the United States and Canada? There are many countries throughout the world with their own rules, regulations, customs, and practices. It is simply not practical to discuss each country individually in these pages, so we will invent a generic foreign country and look at how mechanical licensing and royalties are handled.

The following scenario will apply for most countries of the world, with only the names, percentages, and royalty basis being changed. If you are interested in a specific territory, visit the website of the National Music Publisher's Association (NMPA) at www.nmpa.org and download a PDF file with excerpts from the most recent Income Survey report. These reports are replete with useful information, numbers, charts, and local mechanical income and other information for all significant territories of the world. (The NMPA is to be commended for this fine survey work.)

Our country shall be called Forensia. Within Forensia, the government has set up an organization called FMS, the Forensia Mechanical Society. When a record company wishes to manufacture phonorecords within Forensia, it must pay FMS a royalty levy at the time of manufacture. The levy is analogous to a cigarette or alcohol tax in that the fee is paid by the manufacturer, who eventually passes it on to the consumer as part of the ultimate product cost.

In Forensia, the fee FMS charges is "9.009% of PPD." *PPD* is the *preferred price to dealers*, or the price that most record stores pay to the record company to buy the phonorecords. Coincidentally, according the 12th edition of the NMPA Income Survey, 9.009% of PPD is the same percent charged in Austria, Belgium, Czech Republic, Denmark, Finland, France, Germany, Greece, Hungary, Iceland, Israel, Italy, Lithuania, Netherlands, Norway, Poland, Portugal, Romania, Slovak Republic, Spain, Sweden, and Switzerland, so this example is very typical. In some countries the royalty basis is based not on PPD but on adjusted retail price, an imputed (by estimate or agreement) or actual retail selling price, or some other basis. I know of no countries other the United States and Canada that operate on a fixed currency rate per unit as opposed to some sort of percentage. In some territories the percent and basis are determined by government, by collective bargaining, or by another method. In Forensia, the amount and basis is determined by King Wastrel.

So King Wastrel has now decreed that all of the smaller (read: nontrustworthy or financially fragile) Forensian labels must pay a 9.009% levy on the given PPD to FMS before they can take their CDs out of the pressing plant and distribute and sell them. King Wastrel allows the major Forensian labels (because they are big and therefore honest and trustworthy) to pay their royalties to FMS on a monthly basis in arrears.

As you know, in Forensia, the PPD for CDs is 10.6 spazios. CDs are then marked up and sold in stores to consumers for 15.1 spazios. Doing the math, we see that when 9.009% is levied on 10.6 spazios, 95.495 spaziettes (100 spaziettes, of course, equal 1 spazio) are payable to publishers for each CD manufactured. FMS, our trusty local mechanical society, takes its 15% commission for overhead costs and local political bribes and kickbacks to the King, and then distributes the remaining 81.117 spaziettes to the various publishers whose songs are on the CD. In some instances, the local mechanical society distributes the collected revenue to the music publishers on the basis of the number of a publisher's songs on a given CD in relation to the total number of songs; in other territories, the revenue is distributed based on a proration of playing time.

The only other significant points worth mentioning about foreign mechanical licensing involve what is called *central licensing*. Central licensing means, that, for example, Warner Records does not manufacture records in each country in a geographical area. In Europe, Warner doesn't manufacture the same CD in England, Germany, France, the Netherlands, Spain, Italy, and Scandinavia. That would be too much duplicate effort. Instead, Warner manufactures all the CDs for Europe only in Germany, for instance, and then the German mechanical right society (GEMA) collects all the money for all of the CDs that will be sold throughout Europe.

GEMA distributes the net mechanical income available for distribution to music publishers to all of its sister mechanical right societies in the correct amounts relevant to where the total number of CDs are shipped. This system saves a lot of duplicated energy and function. However, it has also resulted in stupidly detrimental competition among mechanical right societies to lure record companies to manufacture in their territories and subject to their local rates. In other words, Society A offers a 8.5% PPD rate to a record company if it manufactures and centrally licenses within Society A's territory. Society B then bids down its beneficiaries' take-home pay (the mechanical royalty rate) by offering the record company an 8% of PPD rate. Obviously, this bidding war between mechanical right societies in order to maintain or grow market share is not in the best interests of their clients, the music publishers.

Thankfully, in Forensia, King Wastrel kills anyone who underbids his mechanical rate.

Who Gets the Money?

Mechanical royalties are paid to the music publisher. The music publisher then pays the writer the traditional writer's half. If a songwriter also owns his own music publishing company, he can either write a check to himself as the songwriter or, if he is not keeping separate accounts or otherwise maintaining a distinction between the writer and publisher shares, he can just keep the money in one place.

Performance Income

Performance income in the United States derives from radio and television broadcast, closed-circuit music providers such as Muzak, nightclubs, gyms, concert halls, airplane entertainment services, and other places where music is publicly performed. Outside of the United States, the laws in many foreign territories provide for the payment of performance royalties for public performance of music in motion picture theaters.

Performance income may be collected directly by the music publisher from the end user (with a *direct performance license*), but in most cases it is collected by a *performing right society*. Performing right societies act to collectively license and distribute public performance income by means of blanket licenses. The United States is possibly unique in the world in that there are two main performing right societies, ASCAP (American Society of Composers, Authors, and Publishers) and BMI (Broadcast Music, Inc.) and also one smaller but growing society, SESAC (which probably stands for something—oh, OK, the Society of European Stage Actors and Composers).

In most (if not all) other countries, there is only one performing right society, and it is often affiliated with the local mechanical royalty society. For example, in England, the mechanical society, MCPS (Mechanical Copyright Protection Society), has an alliance with the PRS (Performing Right Society). By contrast, JASRAC (Japanese Society for Rights of Authors, Composers, and Publishers) collects, licenses, and distributes mechanical, performance, and other income.

In 1914, shortly after the enactment of the United States Copyright Act of 1909, ASCAP was formed at a restaurant in New

York City by a group of composers, authors, and publishers (including Irving Berlin) for the purpose of licensing public performance of copyrighted musical works. The society was, and continues to be, controlled by its own membership (approximately 175,000 authors, composers, and publishers) who elect the 24 directors. Because ASCAP engages in some sort of collective bargaining, in order to be exempt from antitrust violations, it operates under a "consent decree" agreement under which federal courts oversee and approve its operation.

By 1940, ASCAP was well established and, in fact, so successful at collecting performance royalties from radio stations that the stations themselves started a revolt of sorts. Some stations refused to play any ASCAP-licensed repertoire and would only play public domain material. Ultimately, the broadcasters formed their own competing performing right organization, BMI. Although owned by the broadcasters (this is a very significant difference between ASCAP and BMI), BMI operates as a nonprofit organization for the benefit of approximately 300,000 writers and publishers. Like ASCAP, it operates under a federal consent decree.

How the System Works

But enough of the history. How do performing right societies do their job?

Performing right societies generally operate using the concept of a blanket license. Radio and TV stations (other public performers of music) buy a blanket license from the performing right society. The cost of the license is usually based on gross revenue to the station and is typically around 2.5%. The more advertising the station sells, the more revenue the performing right societies get to collect. Given that there are around 8,500 radio stations in the United States, the total amount collected in blanket license fees can be very substantial.

What do the stations get in exchange for buying a blanket license? They get the right to play anything and everything in that performing right society's repertoire for a period of time. So if a radio station buys blanket licenses from ASCAP, BMI, and SESAC, it can play virtually every published song. This is far easier for the stations than contacting each publisher individually and getting the direct right and license from that publisher to perform its song on the radio. Likewise, the blanket license concept is far easier for music publishers, who don't have to issue licenses to 8,500 radio stations and other public performers of music.

Each of the performing right societies negotiate the cost of blanket licenses based on arguments they make on the relative importance of their repertoire and the percentage of a user's total performance time this repertoire accounts for. For example, ASCAP might tell a given radio station, "Look, last year ASCAP music comprised 43% of the music you broadcast, whereas in the previous year, ASCAP music only made up 39%, so we should get more money for our license this year." Likewise, SESAC might inform a TV station, "We now represent the repertoires of Neil Diamond and Bob Dylan, so you need to pay us a lot more than you did before."

Of lesser importance than the blanket license concept is the *per-program* license. Public performers of music who use little or no music, or who have special agendas or needs, may seek to avail themselves of per-program licensing. For example, talk radio and news stations make very little of their revenue from playing music that people want to hear; instead they rely on interesting (?) talk hosts and stories. It might be more prudent to pay only for the exact music they play, each and every time they play it, than to buy a blanket license. Small independent TV stations would also be good candidates for per-program licenses.

Direct Licenses

Some public performers of music simply refuse to get either blanket or per-program licenses from the performing right societies. In these cases, they actually seek out the original music publishers and negotiate a public performance license directly. ESPN, for instance, likes to obtain public performance licenses directly from publishers and, if the license is not easily obtained, gets a per-program license from the applicable society. The Weather Channel can easily control its musical content and, as of this writing, does not obtain blanket performing right licenses.

Under the terms of the applicable consent decrees under which ASCAP and BMI operate, ASCAP and BMI only obtain *nonexclusive* performing rights to a publisher's repertoire. This means that a publisher also retains the right to issue public performance licenses even though its performing right society represents that same repertoire. The only caveat is that if publishers license a work directly for public performance, they need to tell their performing right societies that they have done this. The reason for this is to prevent a performing right society from instituting a lawsuit against a party for public performance without a license when in fact the user obtained such license directly from the publisher.

OK, So Where Does All the Money Go?

ASCAP, BMI, and SESAC collect enormous sums of money from blanket and performance licenses, which goes into giant funds. From the fund of each organization, operating expenses are deducted, and the remaining sums are distributed to the songwriters and publishers. To give you some actual numbers, in February 2003, ASCAP announced that its total distribution to members for the previous year was $587 million after a 14.8% operating expense deduction. BMI's gross collections were approximately 6% less.

Getting In on the Action

Music publishers and songwriters can join ASCAP, BMI, or SESAC. There are separate performing right society affiliations, and separate agreements, for music publishers and songwriters. Songwriters can only join one United States performing right society, and their affiliation with that society is exclusive. Songwriters are free to move between one society or another upon the expiration of their affiliation term. (In some instances, a BMI writer may elect to leave certain specific works to be licensed by BMI after he has terminated his BMI affiliation and joined ASCAP. He will still be considered a current ASCAP writer even though prior repertoire remains with and is licensed by BMI.)

Publishers, because they may publish works written by ASCAP, BMI, and SESAC songwriters, typically have publishing companies affiliated with two or even three performing right societies. In rare instances, a writer may join one performing right society for the United States and then have a different performing right society represent him for the rest of the world. This might be done, for instance, by a film composer who, while a citizen and resident of Germany, derives a lot of public performance from United States broadcasts and wishes to avail himself of the benefits of direct membership, statements, and payments. Sometimes, too, signing with different societies for U.S. and overseas performing rights is done for tax reasons: to keep otherwise taxable income out of the country of residence.

Here are some specific points to remember with respect to performing right societies.

- A publisher's affiliation on a given work must be the same as a writer's affiliation. An ASCAP publisher cannot publish a BMI writer's work, and a BMI publisher cannot publish an ASCAP writer's work.

- If a song is cowritten by songwriters with differing affiliations, the proportion of affiliation must remain with respect to publishing. If one ASCAP songwriter writes 20% of a song, and two BMI writers each wrote 40% of that same song, the song must be published 20% by an ASCAP company and 80% by BMI companies. (Foreign writers and publishers who are not members of BMI, ASCAP, or SESAC are free to designate which U.S. performing right society will license and collect revenue on a song-by-song basis. In other words, some titles can be licensed through BMI and some through ASCAP or SESAC.)

- The United States performing right societies have reciprocal agreements with their counterparts in other countries. So if you are a member of, say, ASCAP, ASCAP will register your songs internationally for public performance licensing, and ASCAP's sister societies overseas will collect your performing right income and pay it to ASCAP, which will then pay it to you. You do not need to join performing right societies all over the world.

- Performing right income is handled differently than almost any other type of music publishing income. The difference is that the performing right society splits the money due for a song's public performance, paying the writer half directly to the writer and paying the publisher's half directly to the publisher. If you are not clear on writer's half and publisher's half, please reread "Songwriters and Publishers" in the "Overview" chapter. Take a moment to absorb this. Unlike mechanical royalties, where the publisher gets everything and pays half to the writer, ASCAP, BMI, and SESAC think your publisher is untrustworthy scum (he just might be) and want you to receive your half directly before he can get his grubby little hands on it. Accordingly, if you are a self-published writer, you will get two separate (and mostly equal) accountings for the same performances from your performing right society: one for the writer share (Joe Schmoe) and one for the publisher share (Schmoe Songs). They are not double paying you. (You wish.)

  For this reason, income splits are often different for different types of publishing revenue. You might be entitled to 50% of mechanical and synchronization income from your publisher, but entitled to 0% of the public performance income the publisher receives because (ten points if you guessed it) you received your half of the public performance income directly from your performing right society.

- Public performance lives in a world of 200%. This relates to the previous bullet point. The performing right society pays out 100% of half of the performance income to the writer, and pays out 100% of half of the performance income to the publisher. That makes 200%. They could have paid the writer 50% of the whole, and the publisher 50% of the whole, so why do they calculate it this way?

The reason is because they didn't want to get phone calls from guys who say, "Hey, I wrote 100% of this song, how come the statement you sent shows that I'm only getting 50%?"

To try to make it clearer, our foreign friends sometimes use two different designations for performance and other types of income. If you are a 100% publisher of a song, you would get 100% of the mechanical and other income and 100% of the (publisher's share of) performance income in the United States. A frequent foreign convention is to express performing income as a fraction, usually with a denominator of 12. So in the case of Japan, you as a 100% publisher would claim 100% of mechanical and other income, and 6/12 of the performance income. The 6/12 is supposed to make it easier and remind you that this is performance income and that you are only getting half of the whole. In other words, 6/12 is 100% of the publisher's share of performance income. If these conventions further confuse you, just keep telling yourself that they make life easier.

I Still Haven't Been Paid

OK, so ASCAP has a half of a billion dollars sitting in a bank somewhere and you want yours. You've joined ASCAP as a writer and as a publisher, and now you want your money already. How do the performing right societies figure out how much of the blanket and per-program license fees are yours?

The allocation of income is done scientifically by survey. ASCAP, BMI, and SESAC use different methods of allocation, and each swears its system is superior. In the case of radio airplay, stations are monitored. ASCAP uses a system called Mediaguide. BMI uses BDS and MediaBase, and SESAC uses BDS. What all of these systems do is take a scientifically selected group of radio stations and figure out what they are playing. If 20% of the radio stations are playing country music, then 20% of their radio station sampling will be of country stations. If 35% of the stations are hip-hop/rap stations, then 35% of their monitoring will be of hip-hop/rap stations.

These systems then figure out what this scientifically selected group of stations is playing. The MediaGuide system that ASCAP uses, for example, monitors stations right off the air and a computer instantly matches the previously stored electronic "fingerprint" of a song (down to the artist and even particular mix) with what is being played. For each time the station plays your song, you get an appropriate share of the performing right society's blanket and per-program license fee pool. If your big hit song comprises .00125% of the airplay in the country during a given quarter, then you will get .00125% of the royalty pool.

What's On TV?

TV stations (and movie theaters overseas) also pay significant amounts into the license fee pools. This money is allocated according to what are known as cue sheets. A film or TV producer creates a *cue sheet* for a program that lists the name of the production (film name, or TV program name with episode name and number) and then all the music appearing in that program. The cue sheet lists the title of each music cue with the author, the publisher, type of use (theme, background vocal, background instrumental, visual performance, etc.), and the duration of usage. When the film or program is shown on TV, the performing right society digs out the applicable cue sheet and then knows who to credit and pay for the broadcast performance. (Again, in many foreign territories, based on cue sheet information, a pool of income is allocated to music publishers and songwriters out of theatrical box office receipts.)

Because the cue sheet is the basis for royalty payments, it is very important for songwriters and publishers to receive a copy of a cue sheet containing music they own or created. The songwriter/ publisher should review the cue sheet for accuracy and then, although it may be a redundant submission (the producer should have submitted the cue sheet to ASCAP, BMI, and SESAC), submit it to his own performing right society and subpublishers (refer to the chapter on subpublishers) to ensure that anyone who might be in a position to pay him is able to do so.

The performing right societies work on a complete census of all the programs that are broadcast by television networks in the United States. If your music appears in a program that is broadcast on a network, and if a cue sheet that properly reflects your information has been sent to your performing right society, you should definitely receive a payment for the performance. The performing right societies are treating more and more stations in this manner all the time, including many cable channels.

If, however, the program in question airs on "spot" or syndicated TV, it is more difficult for the performing right societies to track usage in this way. Performance royalties from syndicated TV thus tend to be allocated based on a sampling (like radio) rather than a complete schedule-based census.

Do They Monitor My Gym?

Radio and TV we now understand. What about music being played in restaurants, stores, airplanes, aerobic studios, funeral homes, skating rinks, sports stadiums, and kids' gyms? Do the performing right societies monitor these places to see what is being played and to figure out what you're due? No way. Relatively speaking, the fees paid by these users are small. The performing right societies call musical performances in these venues *nonsurveyed*. That means no one is going to check what is being played there. The blanket license (and per-program) fees derived from these music users are nonetheless thrown into the distribution pool. The money gets allocated on the same basis as radio, TV, and other surveyed media in the same proportionate basis as those media. If you are getting .00125% of the total radio (and other surveyed) airplay during a given quarter, then they also throw in .00125% of the pool income relevant to nonsurveyed users.

It may surprise some people to know that an attempt is made to allocate by survey the performance fees paid by concert venues and arenas. Typically, a performing right society obtains a set list (list of songs played, including publishers and writers) either with respect to certain venues spread throughout the country (e.g., Staples Center in Los Angeles, Madison Square Garden in New York) or perhaps by selecting the ten biggest tours in a given year (Rolling Stones, Bruce Springsteen, NOFX). In this way, the societies introduce at least some survey data into the allocation of the performing right fees paid by these venues and tours.

The Enforcer

Every so often you will read in the paper about some poor schlub who is getting sued by ASCAP, BMI, or SESAC. He thought that because he already bought the CD, the music was free to play in his restaurant or boutique or even on the telephone as hold music! (When you buy a CD, you can listen to it in your car or home or wherever, but only for *your personal* use. For our purposes, *your* also includes your family and friends when you play it at home or in the car. But if you want to perform the music contained on the CD in public for profit or other benefit, that is a different animal, and you need a public performance license.)

When ASCAP showed up at the schlub's restaurant and told him he needed a license if he was going to play ASCAP repertoire to create ambiance and help sell food and keep his restaurant trendy and popular and full, he told them where to go. He figured that it was just another shakedown like his payments to "Tony the protection guy" or the health inspector. He was wrong, and now ASCAP has sued him. He will lose the suit, and some lawyer will charge him to mount a hopeless defense. (But then again, he might also get a fair amount of ink in the local Thursday throwaway that he advertises in, so he can feel good about something.)

The amounts charged to these sundry venues by the performing right societies are relatively small, often a nominal amount that barely covers the cost of licensing. But the fees keep everything on the up-and-up while maintaining the legal principle that public performance of other people's music has to be paid for. When a performing right society calls a publisher and asks for a copy of the copyright certificate for "Light My Fire," someone is getting sued for nonlicensed public performance and is about to lose, in that order.

My Performing Right Society Is Better Than Yours

The performing right societies love to argue among themselves as to whose distribution system is best, and they all want to convince you that their system will result in your getting paid more if you please affiliate with them. One of the most ridiculous arguments is that "our survey of stations is twice as big as theirs." If the surveys are large enough and the science and statistics are good, it doesn't matter which survey is bigger. Look at it this way: Let's say a survey of voters shows that 2 million voters, scientifically selected and surveyed out of 5 million total voters, favor a given candidate. If you double the survey size and find that 4 million voters out of 10 million total favor that candidate, you have learned nothing new. At a certain point in time, increasing your sample size does not tell you any new information. It only costs you more money. Likewise if performing right society A pays you 10¢ every time your song gets picked up in its survey, but society B, which has twice as big a survey, only pays you 5¢ each time your song gets picked up in its survey, you will end up getting the same amount in the end because society B will pick you up twice as often but at half the rate. So don't worry about survey size or methodology too much.

Historically, BMI tended to pay its winners (songwriters and publishers with big hits) more money at the expense of the losers. Specifically, BMI had four different bonus plateaus for rewarding songs that attained a lot of airplay. The plateaus were relative (e.g., your song is in the top 10% of airplay for BMI songs this quarter) rather than absolute (you got more than 100,000 airplays), so it was very hard to figure out where you stood. There was a basic rate they paid. Then there were "entry-level bonuses" (1.5 times the normal rate), "mid-level bonuses" (2.5 times the normal rate), and "super-level bonuses" (4 times the normal rate). So if you had a "small" song that got limited airplay, BMI would by necessity be paying you less so that it could pay the guy with the monstrous hit four times what he would ordinarily get.

Effective July 1, 2004, BMI instituted a new system to replace the four-tier bonus model. There are now three royalty payment components: a "current activity" payment, a "hit song bonus," and a "standards bonus." The current activity amount is based upon the actual fees paid by the station that played the song, rather than on a pool of blanket fees. The hit song bonus is for any work that has 95,000 performances in a given quarter. The amount to be allocated for hit song bonuses by BMI is not specified, and may or may not be fixed. The standards bonus is available to works with more than 2.5 million cumulative performances, and at least 25,000 performances in a given quarter. The standards bonus is also cumulative, which means that works with a high combination of current quarter and historical performances earn larger bonuses.

Compared to BMI, ASCAP tends to be more egalitarian: an airplay is worth what an airplay is worth. But ASCAP has instituted a single top-tier bonus as well so that it pays out roughly the same amount of money to an ASCAP hit song as BMI would have otherwise paid out to that same hit song (isn't competition a wonderful thing?).

Competition in the United States between the performing right societies is often intense. From time to time, these organizations try to lure songwriters and publishers from each other and sometimes pay advances for a defection if the artist is important enough and makes a significant difference in the blanket and per-program licenses they can obtain from music users. My own opinion is that in most instances, a writer or publisher should go for the best performing right society and not be seduced by advances, which are basically transitory and not a function of quality.

How does one choose the "best" performing right society? Sometimes this choice is based on who provides you with the most support, encouragement, and assistance, but in most instances it comes down to who will pay you more for your performances. An interesting exercise is to compare payouts on split copyrights. Let's say you have a song that was written 50% by an ASCAP writer and 50% by a SESAC writer. (And of course we remember that we therefore have a 50% ASCAP publisher and a 50% SESAC publisher collecting the publishers' shares.) The song is a big hit and each writer (and publisher) receives his performing right statement from his respective performing right society. Oh, look at this! The ASCAP writer/publisher amount was $50,000 for the quarter, but the SESAC writer got $61,000. Does this really happen? Absolutely.

In my personal experience making such comparisons over many years, ASCAP has outpaid BMI except for a few cases involving big country hits when BMI trounced ASCAP. I can't draw a similar comparison with SESAC because I have only administered two SESAC companies, and no split copyrights were involved. Many people in the industry have had different experiences, though, and in fact I have found BMI to be more accommodating than ASCAP and more likely to respond quickly to a problem or issue. Difficult choices and trade-offs are involved in your choice of performing right society.

Lastly, know that in payment formulas, various weighting factors are applied to payouts, such as types of uses (a TV theme is worth more than a background "car radio playing" type use) and time of broadcast (prime time is better than 3:30 A.M. on Sunday morning), size of market, and other significant factors.

Synchronizations

Unlike mechanical licensing, where there is a statutory rate or customary percentage basis to start from, and unlike performance licensing, where the licenses and rates are almost always handled by a third-party performing right society, synchronization licensing frequently requires a great deal of knowledge, decision making, and negotiating skill from the music publisher. Synchronization licensing and uses are thus among the most interesting and challenging areas in the publishing field.

The most important types of synchronization licenses involve television and motion picture productions. (Advertising often involves synchronizations but will be treated separately in the "Sundry Uses" chapter.) Many types of licenses are used in film and TV production, and the rule of thumb is the more they want, the more they pay. Myriad factors may be introduced into a negotiation, resulting in much different pricing and rates.

Film Factors

Some of the factors a music publisher might consider as part of the decision and quoting process for a motion picture are listed below. It is extremely good business practice to require a potential film licensee to send a written request with as many of these variables spelled out as possible.

- The name of the picture, the stars, the director, the distributors, the studio and/or financiers, the projected film rating, the budget, and a plot synopsis.

- How the film proposes to use your song, including the type of use (background instrumental, background vocal, opening credits, closing credits, repeated theme, etc.) and the duration(s).

- A specific scene description and a few pages of script indicating the proposed use in context.

- The type and duration of rights that you are to be quoting on. Is it for a fixed period of years (five? ten?) or for perpetuity? (As an aside, it is inadvisable to quote for perpetuity since the rights you have under copyright law are not for perpetuity but for a fixed period of years. If you grant rights that you don't have, you could get in trouble. Whenever you see the word *perpetuity*, try to remember to cross it out and replace it with "life of copyright, plus renewals and extensions.") In which media do they want to include the song (movie theaters, television, home video devices, "technology now known or hereinafter devised," etc.)?

- The territory for which the rights are desired (United States, the World, and now, frequently, the Universe).

- Which master recording of your song they will be using (if there is more than one), or if they plan to rerecord the song themselves. Remember, too, that the film production will need to license your musical composition (PA copyright) and license (or create) a master (SR copyright) recording.

- Whether they want the song for ancillary uses ("making of" documentaries or other featurettes, trailers, advertising, sequels, soundtrack albums, etc.).

Of course, before formulating a quote, you should always ask yourself the question: "Is this a film I want this song to be in?" You might not even have to consider any of the foregoing!

Most major studios and film productions will now simply ask you to quote on a *broad rights license*. What they usually mean by this is a worldwide license for a duration of the life of copyright, plus renewals and extensions, covering usage within the *linear film* (as opposed to excerpted outside of the use within the film) in theaters, television, home video devices, future linear motion picture devices or transmission methods, and in-context advertising, in-context promotions, and in-context trailers.

An aside about "in context" is in order here. *In context* refers to uses of a song as it appears within a film. The scene and exact visual images in the same timed relationship that they appear within the motion picture represent an in-context use. If a film uses your song where a man is seen chopping down a tree, an in-context use will always have that same man chopping down that same tree to your song. *Out of context* would be where a production lifts your song as separate music from that scene and then uses it, for example, as a musical bed for a television commercial or theatrical trailer where many other scenes and images are used.

It is common, but by no means an absolute requirement, to grant in-context uses within a broad rights motion picture license. In this way, the studio is free to have its stars go on talk shows and show clips of scenes that include your music, and not have to strip out your background music. The same applies to in-context use within trailers, advertising, and other promotions for the motion picture. The music publisher is cautioned, though, to be possibly redundant by adding the words "in context" in a quote for a license request that asks for "additional use in in-context trailers, advertising, clips, and promotions." Since it is not definitively clear whether the requestor's use of *in-context* is intended to modify just *trailers* or also *advertising, clips,* and *promotions*, it is wise to indicate on the request that you are quoting on "in-context trailers, in-context advertising, in-context clips, and in-context promotions." Once you've had an argument with a film studio as to what *in context* was supposed to modify, you will never forget to make this clarification again.

Broad rights licenses are almost always granted on a flat-fee basis. They pay you once, and that is it. There will be no additional fees for TV broadcast, airplane showings, or home video devices like VHS tapes and DVDs. Also, the fee paid to a record company to license a given master recording of a publisher's song is usually (but not absolutely) on a most favored nations basis with that master. It is rare that a master recording quote is allowed to be higher than a music publisher's corresponding quote. Here's a hypothetical situation in which that might occur: Let's say someone is making a film about the group the Doors and thinking of including only one of their "outside" cover recordings, such as Berthold Brecht's and Kurt Weill's "Whiskey Bar" or Willie Dixon's "Back Door Man." In this instance, the producer might decide that the most important thing relevant to the movie is Jim Morrison singing the song and the Doors playing the music (it's Doors-ness) and not the underlying composition. The producer might want to include only one "outside" song and simply choose "Whiskey Bar" or "Back Door Man" depending on which publisher quotes the lesser amount, while paying the Doors' record company a higher fee for the master.

Fees for broad rights synchronization licenses vary widely. An unknown or little-known song within the body of a major studio motion picture may get anywhere (as a typical range) from $10,000 to $20,000, on an MFN basis with the master recording. Those fees might double if the song is used over credits. A known but nonhit song might fetch from $20,000 to $30,000. A hit song or a standard-type song might obtain from $30,000 to $100,000 or more. These quotes, too, are subject within reason to the size of the film's budget and the fame of its stars and director. A $200 million Spielberg *E.T.* sequel would certainly justify a higher quote than a $500,000 production of *Porky's 12: The Fifth Day After the First Week*.

In my experience, a significant synchronization license of a song not specifically written for a given production is always *nonexclusive*. Music publishers want to retain the right to license their songs to other films and TV productions. An *exclusive* license could be issued, but it would have a hugely deleterious impact on the value of a song if it could never be licensed again.

Sometimes, a film production doesn't want (or can't afford) broad rights and a music publisher is asked to quote on limited rights, or sometimes limited rights with priced options for expanded future uses. Some sample limitations might be a request to quote on: "broad rights for the United States only, with an option to be exercised within two years for use in the film outside of the United

States"; "limited theatrical (50 screens or less) and television media only"; or even a hybrid by territory such as "television and home video for the United States, but television, home video, and theatrical outside of the United States." The expected corollary to the more they want, the more they pay, is the less they want, the less they pay. Lower budget productions often try to carve out the acquisition of rights they don't really need to try to obtain a reduced quote for their immediate needs.

Half the World

A few rules of thumb for quoting on less than broad rights can be useful. The United States is typically treated as "half the world" from a music business standpoint. The rest of the world, often referred to as *ROW*, gets the other half. So a U.S. broad rights license would be priced at about half of what a worldwide broad rights license would cost. If you were granting an option for *ROW* broad rights, you would want to have a limited time period during which the producer had the right to exercise it (two years?), and you would want the total split fee of both the United States and ROW broad rights licenses to be greater than if they paid for the World (or Universe) all at once. (You should get more than the total lump sum cost if they are paying you in two lumps, especially if the second payment isn't guaranteed. A 20% uplift on each half of the whole worldwide fee might be appropriate.)

It is important for a publisher to maintain a respectable minimum value to a copyright. If you license the Doors' "Light My Fire" to one low-budget picture for $10,000, and then try to license it later to a high-budget picture for $200,000, you might find the negotiations are difficult if the studio has somehow found out that you took $10,000 last month from the earlier production. The value of music and the importance of maintaining a copyright's long-term viability is discussed elsewhere in this book.

Out-of-Context Uses

Frequently, once a song's use has been confirmed in a film, a production or marketing department may then want to acquire additional ancillary or out-of-context uses. An ancillary use example might be wanting to use a song as a DVD menu musical background (which is also an out-of-context use). The most common request is for out-of-context trailers and/or TV advertising. This is advertising for the film that may be shown in motion picture theater trailers, or on television, which uses your song as a noncontextural musical bed. The trailer might make use of your song throughout all or a substantial portion of its duration, even though your song may have only appeared within the film for ten seconds or even not at all. It is very common for film studios to want to use music to advertise a film that doesn't even appear within the film.

There are often different budgets, and even sometimes different payers, for out-of-context trailer fees. The production budget is usually responsible for the payment of synchronization fees for songs appearing in the film. Sometimes film synchronization fees are even paid for or partially underwritten by a record company that will be putting out a corresponding soundtrack album. The marketing budget may be paid for out of a different budget entirely, and even if the film production is over budget and flat broke, the marketing budget might be flush with pre-allocated money ready to be spent. Sometimes, for example, in the case of a so-called *negative pickup* where a studio obtains distribution to an independently produced film, the party paying for marketing and advertising isn't the same party that produced the film.

It is not unreasonable to quote the same amount for an out-of-context trailer fee as you got for the song being licensed in the motion picture itself. If they paid you $50,000 to synchronize your song in the film itself, then quoting an additional $50,000 for out-of-context trailers and advertising would also be reasonable. And again, on a most favored nations basis with the copublisher and corresponding master recording, right?

For out-of-context trailer uses in the circumstance where a song doesn't even appear in the film itself, most music publishers elect to treat the situation as a straight advertisement using the song and charge more than if the song were in the film. In other words, the usage is not viewed as supplemental income. Fees for out-of-context usage in trailers and advertising when a song is not in the film it is promoting are often in the range of $40,000 to $100,000 and up, depending on how well the song is known by the public and how well it fits in with the film it would be used to advertise. (The life of a film and its eventual home video release, and the corresponding advertising and marketing windows, are usually very short.) And again, on a most favored nations basis with the copublisher and corresponding master recording, as always, right?

I Ain't Got No Money That I Can Depend On

The bane of your existence as a music publisher just might be the student or independent film maker. The good news at least is that the film schools are teaching new film makers that film music isn't free, and getting them grounded in the licensing process. The bad news is that 50 million (maybe 49 million?) of these people want music licenses and have no money to pay for them. Without exception, they always want the most valuable or special song of your most guarded songwriter, the guy who never approves anything anyway and who hardly ever answers your inquiries in less than two months. Typically it costs you more money to issue a license to these film makers than you get from them, and it takes you more time than you have to spend. In short, the Law of Inverse Effort is in action.

A reasonable compromise, at least for film school students, is a limited *film festival license*. These are usually one- or two-page documents, with a specified term of from one to three years, limiting exhibition only to not-for-profit film festivals, classroom use, and maybe a small number of video copies for friends and family (say, 25 copies?). Fees are typically from $50 to $350. It is important, too, that since you will generally not be wasting your time reading the script and screening the movie, that the license state clearly that it is being granted on a nonprecedential basis (meaning that you won't be required to do it that way again), and that you are under no future expressed or implied obligation to license the work for any additional media, period of time, or other circumstance whatsoever. And once the young film maker starts having her spinster sister-in-law, the maritime law attorney, calling you to negotiate the deal, it's time to cut loose and run.

Independent films are a tougher call. You never know what film is going to be the next *Lost In Translation* or an independent box-office megahit. On the one hand, it would be nice to have a song in a big well-known film; on the other hand, simply "nice" doesn't do it unless you're also getting paid. A step deal clause (as discussed in the chapter on "The Value of Music") might be considered. Typical wording for this sort of clause would be something like:

"If and when the Motion Picture attains gross receipts of $20 million dollars, Producer shall pay to Publisher within 30 days thereafter an additional fee of $10,000. If and when the Motion Picture attains gross receipts of $30 million dollars, Producer shall pay to Publisher within 30 days thereafter a further additional fee of $10,000. Said additional payments are payable based on actual gross receipts whether or not publicly reported, although Publisher and Producer both agree that figures reported in such trade publications as *Variety, Hollywood Reporter,* or advertisements relating to the Motion Picture in such publications shall be deemed accurate."

There's Never Anything On TV

Television music synchronization licenses are similar to film licenses in many ways except the fees are lower and the media requested is usually only TV (and maybe common carriers such as cruise ships and airlines) and possibly home video. Many TV programs don't even make it past a few episodes or ever make it to the point where they are aired outside of the United States. It is very common to get TV synchronization license requests with limited terms and territories. These quote requests are often replete with options that the producer can exercise if and when the show runs past its third episode, gets sold overseas, ends up on home video, etc.

A typical request might be for a quote for two years, U.S. and Canada, for all television media. Again, many of the bullet points discussed above with respect to film licensing are applicable. A fee in the $2,500 to $6,500 range might be appropriate. A 24-month option might be requested for the right to obtain all television rights, worldwide, for the life of copyright and renewals. A supplemental fee (make sure it is very clear that this is in addition to the initial fee and not instead of it) in the $5,500 to $8,000 range might be appropriate. A fee for unlimited manufacture of home video devices (referred to as a *video buyout*) is typically in the $8,000 to $12,000 range.

For established TV shows that have passed the point in their existence of sweating whether they will be picked up for another season, the producers often obtain worldwide television and home video rights quotes. *The Simpsons* is a good example of the type of show that would need long-term television rights and also home video rights. When everything is licensed, paid for, and quoted up front, a typical use for all television, worldwide, for the life of copyrights and renewals might go for $8,000 to $12,000. Home video rights in the form of a buyout would also be in the $8,000 to $12,000 range, and you might give the producers a little break if they pay for the TV rights and the video buyout not as an option but at the same time. And what is our mantra? Most favored nations with the copublisher and master recording. You may even wish to extend your most favored nations requirement to include all songs and master recordings in the program or episode.

Video Licenses

There are many types of home video programs. Most motion picture licenses already include home video rights as part of the initial flat fee. Likewise many, but not all, TV synchronization licenses make provisions for a home video (DVD, VHS, etc.) flat-fee buyout. The types of programs that aren't covered in this way are discussed here.

Such programs would typically consist of material that has a more limited audience. Examples might be for a Discovery or National Geographic channel program on fruit bats that will be released on DVD for all of 5,000 people to buy. A video producer might then offer a lower than usual video buyout due to the smaller audience, perhaps with some sort of unit cap and time limit, for instance, $2,500 for up to 25,000 units distributed for up to seven years. An alternative might be a royalty-based approach with a per-unit fee of anywhere from 9¢ to 14¢, maybe with a smaller ($500 to $1,000?) advance. This approach, analogous to a video mechanical license, is also used frequently in home video programs where the music is more significant, such as concert video DVDs. (Because the audio-only statutory rate is 8.5¢, a publisher really wouldn't want to quote less than that penny rate given that an audiovisual use is an enhanced "better" use and should cost more.)

It Was Here a Second Ago

Some types of visual synchronized uses are termed *ephemeral*. The copyright act provides for what are called ephemeral uses without the permission of the copyright owner. Ephemeral uses are generally "live" or "live tape delay" type uses where the exploitation is made spontaneously and the necessity of obtaining advance permission would place an undue or impossible burden on the music user.

The only income the writer and publisher receives for an ephemeral use is performance income collected by ASCAP, BMI, or other performing right society.

Some recognized examples of ephemeral uses are the incidental background broadcast use at a baseball or football game, live news program uses, and parade broadcasts. *Saturday Night Live, Tonight,* and *Late Night with David Letterman* may also be considered ephemeral uses for which no advance permission is legally required. (Note, however, once the original programs are rebroadcast—such as on *The Best of Saturday Night Live* or *The Best of Letterman*—they are no longer ephemeral uses and the appropriate party must obtain a synchronization license!)

There are also gray cases that producers claim are ephemeral, but these may not meet certain legal criteria. Many soap operas and broadcast news magazines, for instance, try to squeak by as ephemeral users. A music publisher sufficiently concerned with this matter might wish to retain a copyright attorney to handle and examine the legal issues more thoroughly.

That's BS! No, PBS

Songwriters and publishers sometimes get upset when they see their works synchronized on PBS shows without permission. Guess what? They don't need your permission. Congress has granted PBS the equivalent of a compulsory synchronization license (refer to the chapter on mechanical licensing if you don't remember what compulsory licensing is). PBS may use any of your works that have been publicly distributed without your permission *as long as they comply with the copyright laws on compulsory synchronization licensing.* The government wanted to help public, not-for-profit broadcasters and gave them this gift. PBS pays a very small fee for each such use according to a schedule determined by law. Once a year, after your song has been used by PBS, they track you down, ask you to confirm your ownership, and then send you a check. The amount isn't very big, but you've helped support public broadcasting in your own little way, like it or not.

Those Foreigners Did What?

The usual convention is that synchronization licenses are issued in the territory where the production is based even if the license is to cover the entire world. United States music publishers typically employ various parties to represent their repertoire throughout the world. These foreign representatives are called *subpublishers*. It is customary for the original publisher to grant various subpublishers the right, subject to the original publisher's approval, to grant worldwide synchronization license for works produced within the subpublisher's territory.

Thus, a film produced in England that requires a worldwide synchronization license typically contacts the applicable English subpublisher. Likewise, worldwide synchronization licenses for productions based in Japan look to Japanese subpublishers, and so forth. Almost all films and TV shows shown in the United States are made in the English language and are thus the primary concern of most United States music publishers. Unfortunately, foreign subpublishers often take a more laissez-faire approach to synchronization licenses for films and TV shows that are in foreign languages and are unlikely ever to be seen in the United States.

Throughout the world outside of the United States, English-language films and TV programs are produced primarily in the U.K., Australia, and New Zealand. Unlike in the United States, where $100 million to $200 million budgets are common, most foreign English-language films and programs are made with more modest budgets. Consequently, synchronization fees for English-language films produced outside of the United States also tend to be more modest. Nonetheless, if a foreign English-language film has significant stars and directors and will be opening "wide" (i.e., 1,000 to 2,000 screens or more) in the United States, there is no reason why the synchronization fee charged by the applicable subpublisher to the foreign English-language film production shouldn't be the same as if the film were a domestic production.

Foreign-language films wishing to use a publisher's music usually get a much better price because the exposure and distribution that their film (or TV program) will receive is far more limited. The best advice as to what a synchronization license should cost in a foreign territory is often received from the original publisher's local agent, the subpublisher.

In the mechanical licensing chapter, we talked about how in some ways, local mechanical right societies are detrimentally affecting their principals' rights by competing over central licensing agreements. Another way that some foreign mechanical and/or performing right societies are hurting their principals and eroding the value of their property is by offering film and/or TV producers blanket licenses covering synchronizations.

In the United States, music publishers ordinarily have the right to say, "No, I don't want my song to be in that TV show, and I won't issue a synchronization license." However, due to blanket synchronization license arrangements, some TV and film producers in some territories automatically include the publisher's work in a program without the need for any formal permission. All the producers have to do is pay the specified fee or tariff to the local rights society where the original publisher's works have been registered.

For example, neither the BBC or Channel 4 in England require any formal approval to synchronize your music; they just have to pay the amount specified by the local mechanical right society, MCPS. Besides unconscionably denying the publisher the right to review and decline or approve a proposed use, such rates tend to be far less than would be negotiated in an arm's length agreement. In fact, the specified rates tend to be given as rate per second, such as £8/second. The characteristics of neither the particular song nor the production are considered. Additionally, such blanket-granted synchronization licenses tend to be overly broad and often allow the programs to be shown outside of the territory of jurisdiction of the local society, including in the United States, and also often include home video devices.

Why would a foreign rights society do this? Simply because it is an easy, automatic way to collect (and commission) greater income. It would be much better in these situations if the original publisher's local subpublisher, not the local rights society, controlled synchronization licensing. The local subpublisher has the original publisher's interests at heart; the subpublisher wants to keep the original publisher's account by keeping him happy, and has coincident interests in the long-term value of a copyright.

I am aware of some publishers in England who are now not registering works with the local mechanical right society, MCPS, for this very reason. Instead, these publishers are directly collecting mechanical income from the applicable record label (as we do here in the United States) and not through a mechanical rights society. By not registering these works with MCPS, the publishers are not subjecting their works to blanket synchronization licenses and the often embarrassingly low fees charged for them. Instead, these publishers are retaining approval over the uses of their works in audiovisual media.

Least Favored Nations

Another aside about most favored nations quotes is in order here. A few of the studios have decreed that it is now their policy not to license songs on a most favored nations basis. Or to grant limited most favored nations protection only with respect to the copublisher and/or corresponding master recording. Just remember, though, that these "written in stone" corporate policies are arbitrary, unilaterally determined, and not to your benefit. You may well have your own corporate policy that says you only issue licenses on Thursdays, or that you won't deal with people who have the letter *e* in their first name, or even that *you only grant licenses that include most favored nations protection.* You are the only one who owns and can license this particular song (unless you have a copublisher on a split copyright). Your song is unique in the world, and why should their corporate policy trump your corporate policy? Just because they're bigger than you?

If you have a genuine concern that the studio may be paying more for other similar songs and uses in the same program, or if you simply want to make sure that they are not, you may *not* want to give on this point. Being branded as difficult or unreasonable (meaning, you won't do exactly what they want you to do) can result in a publisher having fewer or no new requests from a given TV or film studio, so be careful. These (and other similar) battles should be fought only when the stakes are significant and when the principle truly matters to you, a songwriter, or client. Arriving at a mutually satisfactory compromise is preferable.

The only time I feel strongly about going to the wall on a most favored nations dispute is when an original quote and/or confirmation letter was made on that basis. Trying to remove most favored nations wording once the formal licensing process gets underway is an underhanded and dishonest thing to do. (It's right up there with, "Oh, you wanted floor mats with the car?") If your accepted quote included MFN wording, then some corporate lawyer citing "corporate policy written in stone" has no legal, moral, or ethical right to deprive you of a very valuable (but nonfinancial) component of the deal once licensing has begun. This kind of maneuver also means, in many cases, that someone else is getting a better deal than you and they don't want you to know it.

Sometimes all it takes to make you feel like you're getting something in return for giving up the MFN benefit is to have a few thousand dollars more thrown in. This way, the studio can feel big and strong and know that its almighty arbitrary corporate policy has withstood yet another unworthy assault.

A Few More Do's and Don'ts

A publisher should not give an indefinite open-ended quote for any type of synchronization license. A given quote should always have an expiration date. Legally speaking, options are recognized as having an economic value. If you are giving someone an option to use your song ten years from now, you should be compensated for that option. Giving quotes with a 60- or 90-day period of acceptance is a good way to protect a copyright. If the decision has not been made on whether or not to use a song, or if the production or postproduction has not been completed, a publisher can always agree to requote a proposed use or agree to extend the term for which the prior quote is valid.

When giving a quote (and all requests and quotes should always be in writing), it is a good idea to indicate that a given quote is "subject to a signed written license, and payment of the specified fees." Don't blur the line and have the written quote serve as an integrated (complete) license form in and of itself. The reason is because a good license form will have many terms other than the basic licensed media, uses, terms, and fees that will be beneficial to both parties. These may include the specification of legal venue (California, New York, English Law, etc.); restrictions on editing or arranging a song to fit the picture; and requirements that the producer prepare and submit an accurate cue sheet to the publisher and applicable performing right societies (so the publisher can receive performance income), provide for mutual indemnifications, and provide for screen credits of the writer and/or publisher; and many other very important terms.

In the case of a song owned partially (say, 50%) by a publishing company, it is also advisable for a given quote to be not only on a most favored nations basis with the corresponding master recording but with the copublisher. You don't want the production to pay you less for the license of your half of the song than he is getting for the license of the other half of the song. Likewise, if the song is split unequally, you want the most favored nations to apply on a prorated basis. For this reason, many music publishers give a quote with the notation that "quote is based on 100% of copyright, prorated for our share" to indicate both most favored nations intent and to remind the licenser that they don't possess all the ownership in a given song.

Please remember, too, that fees given in this chapter are subjective opinions. Paradigms and norms change quickly and until you develop an ongoing and dynamic feel for pricing, you should consult with others more knowledgeable of current industry norms.

Confirmation Letters

Productions often send music publishers confirmation letters detailing the terms of a synchronization quote that has been given by the publisher. It is a good idea to carefully review these confirmation letters for accuracy, to make appropriate changes where necessary, and to indicate again that the quote given is "subject to a signed written license, and payment of the specified fees." The confirmation letters are often prepared by music clearing houses and not the producers themselves. The unfortunate reality is that many of these music clearance houses are very amateurish, unknowledgeable, dishonest, and sloppy. (But other than that, they're fine.) The confirmation letters they send you usually contain a statement to the effect that they are "proceeding in reliance" of your quote, and thus while they are trying to legally bind you to an offer to license, they are doing so before they themselves have confirmed that they will in fact be using your song. Legally speaking, they are trying to protect themselves against potential licensing problems through *detrimental reliance*. Within commonsense limits, it is reasonable for them to want to have you on the hook to agree to license a song to them even though they aren't necessarily on the hook to use the song until the film is finished, edited, and ready for theatrical distribution. But this is specifically why you will again want to verify the terms on the confirmation letter and to have it be subject to a formal written signed license (to be negotiated in good faith) and the receipt of the payment of the sums you have quoted.

Sundry Uses

The three main types of licensing and income we have just explored—mechanical, performance, and synchronization—comprise the most important and common areas of interest for the majority of music publishers. This chapter surveys other common types of licensing and their normal terms and conditions.

Advertising

By far the most important type of sundry music license in today's market is advertising. There are many songwriters and publishers who eschew advertising altogether, many who embrace it wholeheartedly, and some who allow it only under specific circumstances. Those parties who do not wish to use their songs in advertising frequently cite the fact that the songs they create have special meaning and importance to them, and that they don't want to pervert that meaning by using songs to sell products. Some of these principled writers have turned down millions and millions of dollars. I personally have witnessed a client decline a $22 million (publishing and master) five-year worldwide multimedia advertising campaign, solely because the writers and publishers did not want to be in the business of selling "big gas-guzzling cars."

More often, songwriters and publishers who have been reticent to allow the use of their songs in commercials slowly move toward acceptance of advertising licenses when compelling reasons can be given to override the basic objection. Such reasons might include a song's use in marketing environmentally "green" products and services that help humanity. Recently one of my clients, who would previously rather have died than issue an advertising license, agreed to do so because, in the particular case, the commercial would indirectly help more than 30,000 workers to retain their jobs. Another similarly situated client, for whom advertising licensing had been unthinkable, was willing to allow the use of an important copyright in a commercial for solar energy products.

Finally, there are those who either are not so emotionally attached to their songs, or feel that having the song in the public's mind and ear might help their careers—or at least their checkbooks. Certain artists have indeed used advertisements to help propel or revive stalled careers, or simply to bask in renewed public exposure. Songwriters such as Sting, Michael McDonald, and Steve Miller have publicly acknowledged the benefits from advertising campaigns featuring their music.

There really isn't a right or wrong response to an advertising request. This is a subjective issue that's affected by, among many other things, financial pressures and realities.

The most typical advertising campaign license request is for a national (United States) one-year TV campaign. Typical fees (and there are many cases where fees are not typical) for such a campaign are in the $175,000 to $500,000 range (just for publishing). Determining factors are the size of the company doing the advertising and the likely campaign budget, frequency of exposures, the unique suitability of the song to the product or campaign, and the desire of the advertiser balanced against the reticence (if any) of the songwriter and publisher. There might also be additional media (such as radio, print, and website) advertising thrown into the picture, and those media would raise the quoted price typically by 10% to 30%.

Advertising agencies also try to negotiate lower music fees by limiting the TV commercials to "spot television," "regional television" (example: only five western states), or "13-week advertising cycles." Fees for this nature of advertising are more likely to be in the $75,000 to $125,000 range. Granting this type of license is like being a little bit of a virgin. Once your song is out there, people don't know that it is only on a spot, regional, or limited-term basis, and this license may very well preclude other advertising opportunities that otherwise may have come to light. If a song has been sitting around for two decades and no one has wanted it for a commercial, go for it. On the other hand, if you receive inquiries about a specific song's availability for advertising every few months (one of the first things they always ask you is what else the song has been used for and when), then it might be prudent not to knock out a big national spot in favor of a low-budget regional oil and lube commercial.

For a worldwide deal, the fees discussed above might be doubled. There is also an acceptance within the advertising industry that certain products carry a stigma, and that the fees discussed previously for these particular stigma products might be double, triple, or even higher compared with the fees discussed above. Such stigma products might include beer, hard liquor, feminine hygiene products, dog food, kitty litter, toilet paper, condoms, hemorrhoid or rectal itch products, etc. *Parody lyrics*, where the song's original lyrics are changed to better suit the product or campaign, can also raise the fair market value of an advertising license by 25% to 50% or more.

Licensing for radio advertising alone, for one-year campaigns, will more likely be in the $60,000 to $120,000 range, but again is subject to many of the factors discussed above.

Outside of the United States, at least in major industrial nations such as Japan, England, Germany, France, Scandinavia, Spain, Australia, and Italy, fees for one-year campaigns related to major products and well-known songs are typically in the $35,000 to $100,000 range (just for publishing rights), but the original publisher's local subpublisher is a good source of information concerning normal local terms and rates. European subpublishers, in particular, are more likely to tie the fees into a percentage of the total campaign budget (including media buys), frequently around the 5% figure.

Video Games

If you are able to get past the content of many of the games and can swallow the insulting money currently being offered (contrasted with the obscene money being made by the game companies), or if you feel you want the exposure, you might want to consider video game licensing. I have from time to time obtained publishing fees in the $20,000 to $50,000 range and consider this range fair to both the licenser and licensee. Video game companies once in awhile will also agree to a royalty per unit along with an advance.

To me, the flat-fee buyouts in the $2,000 to $5,000 range that are typically offered seem entirely too low unless you truly believe that being exposed to this new audience (who is more interested in games and computers than music and concert tickets) is a step toward building or revitalizing a songwriting or music career. If the offer is nonetheless enticing, you might as well hang out a shingle that says, "We'll take any offer for anything from anyone."

Print

Printed sheet music, songbooks, and album-matching folios comprise the bulk of the written music sold in the United States. There are only a few companies left in this segment of the market, among them Warner Bros. Publications, Hal Leonard Corporation, Cherry Lane Music Company, and Music Sales Corporation.

Advances are common, and may be based on either a period of years or a number of albums. A typical advance for a matching folio for a newly released CD is in the $10,000 to $35,000 range, with new groups and talent more likely to be at the lower end. Songbooks of guitar gods also seem to fetch more.

The royalty rates offered are pretty much the same everywhere, and as long as you insist that your rates are on a most favored nations basis, you'll be fine. Typically, the MFN rates are as follows.

- 20% of the suggested retail selling price of each piano/vocal sheet music.

- 15% of the suggested retail selling price of other individual sheets (easy piano, piano solo, guitar, etc.).

- 10% of educational, band, choral, and multi-artist books (*Best of the '60s, Justin's Favorites from the '90s, etc.*). Expect to be prorated by the number of songs in multi-artist books.

- 12.5% of songbooks such as personality folders (e.g., *The Best of the Doors*) and album-matching folios (The Doors, *L.A. Woman*). It is also standard to add a 5% royalty for the use of the artist's name, image, and likeness (*NIL royalty*). So if you, the publisher, have these rights to grant, throw them in. If the project is a Barbra Streisand or Celine Dion album-matching book, and you only control the songs and not Barbra or Celine (does anyone, really?), then you can't grant this right and won't get the 5% NIL royalty.

- 75% of net receipts from third-party sublicenses. An example is when your print company licenses two lines from your song as a chapter-heading epigram in a novel.

There may also be special provisions for lyric-only editions, unbound editions, etc. Generally, these are not economically significant and as long as you proceed on a most favored nations basis, you'll be no worse off than anyone else.

Finally, remember that the print companies are all now becoming more active in downloadable and online sheet music sales, and the paradigm will no doubt be changing as a result. Keep your eyes open.

Ringtones

Programmable telephone ringtones are a meaningful source of income for music publishers, with (at this writing) $3 billion in annual fees paid. I am currently quoting as follows, on a most favored nations basis with all other publishers in a given service:

- Audio only: the greater of 10¢ per song, or 10% of the amount charged by the ringtone provider.

- Audio with graphics: the greater of 20¢ per song, or 10% of the amount charged by the ringtone provider.

As the performing right societies also collect public performance income for ringtone uses, it seems advisable to withhold public performance rights in ringtone licenses. It is also advisable to enter into these new technology licenses on an experimental nonprecedential basis. Terms should be short (perhaps one year) or otherwise cancelable at will on 60 days' notice.

Karaoke

Karaoke licensing has been around longer than ringtone licensing. There are a lot of sleazy companies in this field, so be careful. These licenses are nonexclusive, so you can license to lots of different (reputable) companies. Since karaoke involves lyric reprints, make sure that your karaoke agreement doesn't conflict with any rights you have granted in a print deal. Normal or typical terms that you want to have on a most favored nations basis are:

- Term: 7 years.

- Territory: World excluding Japan (JASRAC will collect and pay your subpublisher a lot more than you'll get here in the United States).

- Royalty rate: 14¢ a unit for the first 3.5 years; 17¢ a unit for the second 3.5 years.

- Advance: 5,000 units at 14¢ = $700.

- Fixing fee: Nonrecoupable additional fee of $350.

Foreign Translations

Publishers are frequently approached by foreign writers and publishers interested in doing foreign-language versions of a song. I do not generally approve of versions where only the original melody is retained and the lyrics relate to a completely different subject than the original ones. I prefer that foreign-language versions of songs be, as much as possible, direct and literal translations of the original sentiment expressed, with reasonable allowance for local idiom. Some other terms and requirements to consider:

- The new lyrics should be a work made for hire (which means they are completely owned and controlled by the original publisher), so you are not gaining a copublisher, cowriter, or partner in the song's ownership by permitting the new version. The copyright in the new version (a derivative work) should be in the same name(s) as the original song.

- Should the translator/adapter receive any writer or publisher share of the income (related to the new version only)? Because it can be a nightmare distinguishing which version of the song (the original or the translated one) is earning the income, you may simply decide that the translator/adapter gets nothing. (It's your choice.) In many cases, if the guy doing the translation is also in a group that is recording the new foreign version and is making artist royalties anyway, it won't be a big deal to him. If the translator/adapter is, in your consideration, benefiting the copyright by exposing it to a new audience (for example, a Japanese superstar wants to redo a song that flopped for you in the United States), perhaps you would allow him a 10% to 15% translator/adapter's share (on the new version only).

- Mechanical licensing should be at the full local rate.

- The new translator/adapter should indemnify the original writers and publishers against any third-party or infringement claims in case something he added to the new version of the song wasn't his to add.

- There should be a written and signed agreement that specifies your local law for venue and disputes.

- There should be a specific requirement that the new lyrics are not offensive, defamatory, or profane, or that they do not in any way demean or lessen the value of the original copyright.

- If the song is a split copyright, the permission should be contingent upon the translator/adapter receiving permission from your cowriters or copublishers, and on the same terms, prorated.

Sometimes people may want to create same-language adaptations of your existing copyrights, such as a parody version of "My Sharona" called "My Bologna." This is almost the same situation as a translated/adapted foreign version, and you should use the same considerations in arriving at a decision on whether to approve it, and at what terms. The bottom line in both instances should be, "Is it good for the song?"

Samples

Sampling (the interpolation of existing copyrights into new ones) also creates derivative works. Sampling may involve both songs and master recordings and where it does, the sampler requires both a master sample license and a composition (publishing) sample license.

Most sampling requests come from the rap, hip-hop, and R&B worlds. When considering a sample request, it is important to obtain and review a transcription of the lyrics or rap in order to make an informed decision. The decision of the original publisher is binding but also entirely subjective. The sampler might only be using three of your notes, or four of your words, but if those three notes or four words comprise (in your opinion) the bulk of what is good about the new song, you might require 80%, 90%, or more of the new derivative copyright to be owned by the original publishers. As another example, if your song comprises only a musical bed for completely new (and acceptable) lyrics, you might feel a 50/50 split is fair.

Most sample licensing involves joint ownership of the newly created copyright, and often an advance. If the sampler is subject to a controlled composition clause in his recording agreement, the mechanical rate payable to the sample also has to be addressed, not just the percentage claimed of the new work. Sometimes sample licenses are also done on a flat-fee basis.

Sampling license agreements should always be in writing. They tend to be very long and complex and are often subject to our Law of Inverse Effort. (If you get into a dispute, gangsta rappers can be the wrong people to have pissed off at you.) The sampling agreement should always attach as an exhibit a tape or CD serving as an audio demonstration of how you have agreed that your copyright will be interpolated into the new work. If you don't do this, greater or different portions of your work than you thought you were licensing might end up in the new work. Make provisions, too, as to what will happen if someone else samples the newly created work (embodying your copyright) into a third work (a sample of a sample). Always make sure that there is an indemnification in favor of the original writers and publishers against any third party or infringement claims for new material added to your original work. If you are only a copublisher of the sampled work, you should require that your copublisher also agrees with the proposed use and terms.

That's Not Fair—or Is It?

Special attention and further research might be in order for those particularly interested in sampling and parody. Recent court decisions have effectively carved out *de minimus* (minor, in legal speak) uses as not requiring sample clearance. Further, §107 of the copyright act provides for certain types of *fair uses*, for which no license or permission is required. For example, if I am writing a scholarly book about the '60s and the war in Vietnam, and I want to include an analysis or criticism of Neil Young's song "Ohio," which is about the National Guard's killing of four antiwar protestors at Kent State, I can legally do so (as long as such use of the lyrics falls within fair use constraints). Free speech trumps copyright law. Copyright law (§107 again) is not intended to stifle free speech, and specifically states that fair use "for purposes such as criticism, comment, news reporting, teaching (including multiple copies for classroom use), scholarship, or research is not an infringement of copyright." So if you want to quote and mock bad song lyrics in a review, you can.

The four factors that are listed in the statute as to what constitutes fair use are:

- The purpose and character of the use, including whether such use is of a commercial nature or for nonprofit educational purposes.

- The nature of the copyrighted work.

- Amount and substantiality of the portion used in relation to the copyrighted work as a whole.

- The effect of the use upon the potential market for or value of the copyrighted work.

What this all means is that you now have a bunch of rather (well, let's be blunt) murky and independent conditions and factors that the courts get to interpret (or misinterpret, depending on the case). There's plenty of case law on this, much of it with narrow meanings that people want to apply broadly to their own benefit. Fair use claims and defenses thus require great care and understanding.

New Technologies

New technology is developing at a blistering pace. When I tell my kids that there were no color TVs, cell phones, microwave ovens, push button phones, fax machines, cassette decks, videotape recorders, DVD players, video games, personal computers, or Viagra when I was a kid (and I'm not *that old*), they look at me like I came from a different planet. (Yeah, and people hadn't walked on the moon yet, and there were only 48 states.) There are already competing new home audio formats, SACD and DVD-Audio, and Dad hasn't finished replacing his old 12-inch vinyl records with CDs yet.

Bearing in mind, therefore, that some details in this book may be obsolete before it gets into print (disregard all the numbers or double them!), how do you deal with whatever new technologies come wailing across your little copyright world? Safe advice is to let others go first. Why should you be the guinea pig? Once you see what works for them and what doesn't, and how they have been burned, then you can jump in. But that caution could also prevent you from enjoying a great opportunity before the rest of the world catches on.

You can protect yourself by making short-term most favored nations deals for new technologies that you can get out of if the paradigm takes a rapid twist on you. Long-term deals for developing and emerging technologies can be dangerous. You can also tie the new technology deals to something you already know. For example, I am frequently asked to issue *digital phonograph delivery* (or DPD) licenses. These uses are a lot like mechanical uses, except that the end user gets delivery electronically and saves the music locally in some digital storage device instead of buying a physical phonorecord. (Apple's iTunes is one such DPD service.) The DPD license form I use thus follows the same general course as a mechanical license, requiring payment on the basis of DPDs made and distributed, and requiring a minimum royalty rate floor equal to the statutory mechanical rate at the date of delivery; and should the Copyright Arbitration Royalty Panel of the U.S. Copyright Office authorize a higher DPD rate, then that rate instead applies. The license form is also on a most favored nations basis with all other music publishers. It is deemed to be experimental and not prejudicial to any future position on how DPD licensing will be handled for any further use of the given composition, or for any other compositions.

These protections and reservations allow purveyors of new technology to progress, while simultaneously providing protections for the music publisher and assurances that if industry standards or statutory law improves upon the current business model, the licenses too will advance correspondingly.

Subpublishing

Subpublishers represent publishers and their repertoires in foreign territories. Some music publishers, mostly the multinational companies such as Warner Bros., Sony-BMG, Universal, and EMI, own and operate their own subpublishing offices in various territories throughout the world. While this is an advantage for the companies, it may not be an advantage for the company's clients.

Most publishers employ subpublishers in various territories of the world. Canada is usually, but not always, excluded from subpublishing coverage for United States publishers because of its proximity and the ease of dealing with Canadian companies from the United States. (If you're a music publisher in New York, for instance, you're probably closer to a Canadian record company than to a record company in Los Angeles, and Canadians are friendlier.) Some music publishers hire one multinational firm to represent them throughout the world. Others go on a territory-by-territory basis, hiring the best subpublishers they can find in each territory.

In actuality, each country of the world does not need to be covered. There are many countries of the world where either (practically speaking) copyright obligations are not recognized, or where the income deriving from music copyrights is so small that the cost of collecting your money is higher than what you would get. Many countries are assembled into more manageable territorial groupings. It is thus possible to cover most of the world by having between 15 and 20 subpublishing deals in place. Setting up and maintaining this number of deals can be a lot of work. However, there are clear advantages to picking the best subpublisher in each territory as opposed to making a deal with one preassembled grouping, which may have weaker offices in one country and stronger ones in another. Having individual direct deals also maintains a direct sense of accountability and responsiveness to the original publisher, while dealing with one central office does not.

The following are the most typical groupings:

- Australia, New Zealand, Fiji Island, and the trust territories of New Zealand, Papua, and Western Samoa.

- The United Kingdom of Great Britain, Ireland, Scotland, and PRS territories excluding Canada, Australia, and New Zealand.

- South Africa, SAMRO territories including Transkei, Bophuthatswana, Venda, Ciskei, SW Africa (Nambia), Lesotho, Botswana, Swaziland, and Zimbabwe.

- Belgium, Netherlands, Luxembourg, excluding Radio Luxembourg and Radio Europe #1.

- Spain and Portugal.

- Sweden, Norway, Denmark, Iceland, Finland, and Estonia, Latvia, and Lithuania.

- France, SACEM territories excluding Luxembourg but including Radio Luxembourg and Radio Europe #1.

- Germany, Austria, Switzerland, Romania, the former Soviet Union (except Estonia, Latvia, and Lithuania), Bulgaria, Poland, Albania, the former Yugoslavia, Hungary, and the former Czechoslovakia.

- Italy and Vatican State.

- Japan and Mandate Islands.

- Greece.

- Mexico.

- Far East, including Hong Kong, Singapore, Thailand, Korea, Taiwan, and Malaysia.

- Israel.

- Argentina, Uruguay, Chile, Paraguay, and Bolivia.

- Brazil.

A Good Subpublisher

Music publishing, as a field, is filled with intricacies and complications. The best music publishers are well suited to dealing with myriad details, deadlines, and regulations. Organization, efficiency, and attention to detail; strong mathematic, verbal, and negotiation skills; honesty; and dependability are among the most important characteristics of a music publisher. So, too, are these the qualities to look for in a subpublisher. It also helps if the subpublisher communicates well in English, if that's the only language you know.

It has been said that a good subpublisher is one who answers your letters, faxes, and e-mails quickly. While there may be some truth to this adage, it is important to remember that the correlation between speed of reply and subpublishing quality is not one of causality but one of association. Efficient businesses are on top of things and deal with the tasks at hand promptly, but forcing a poor-quality subpublisher to answer correspondence within 24 hours of receipt doesn't make its fundamental weaknesses go away. So look for speed of reply, but also look deeper.

One of the best ways to find a good subpublisher is to talk to other music publishers. The size of a subpublishing operation is not necessarily important. Further, some publishers prefer independently owned and operated subpublishers. Multinational companies are in business both as publishers and subpublishers, and they might take a fancy to one of your catalogs or songwriters. There are situations in which your subpublishing service provider might turn out to be a competitor, and you should take this possibility into account.

Let's Make a Deal

Making a deal with a subpublisher is generally easy. Most foreign countries have far less of a legal culture than the United States, and usually you will be dealing with the subpublishers themselves and not foreign lawyers.

The typical initial term for a subpublishing deal is three years, with extensions thereafter in one-year increments. The smallest music publishing catalogs might attain an 85%/15% split with a subpublisher. Large, more significant catalogs will get a 90%/10% split, and extremely important and prestigious catalogs may even get a 95%/5% split. In general these splits apply to all types of income. Cover recordings and foreign film and TV placements solicited by and secured through the subpublisher's own direct efforts are generally rewarded with higher splits. Money that is earned *but uncollected* in foreign territories by the original publisher is also referred to as *black box* (or *suspense*) *income* and eventually gets distributed to all the publishers whose works were properly registered and collected in that territory as a kind of bonus. Depending on your clout, you may be able to get a subpublisher to agree to pay you a proportionate share of the black box income he receives.

If advances are being given by the subpublisher against future earnings, the split is usually between 85%/15% and 75%/25%, and the performance split may be doubled so that the subpublisher is getting an imputed commission on the writers' half of performance income (which is paid directly to the songwriter and does not pass through the subpublisher's hands). Where advances are taken, it is also typical that the agreement has automatic one- or two-year post-term extensions if the advances given are not earned out at the end of the initial three-year term.

Many territories require that foreign taxes be deducted from your earnings before your subpublisher sends them to you in the United States. Among these are Italy, Spain, the Far East (varies by country), Australia, and New Zealand. Usually, the amount is no more than 10%, and you should expect to get a tax certificate at the end of the year that may get you tax credits on your United States income tax return. Check with your tax professional. Other countries allow your income to be paid to you without any local tax deduction, although you may have to fill out exemption request forms, and such forms might have to be signed by your bank, certified by the Internal Revenue Service, or accompanied by documentation provided to you by the Internal Revenue Service. Your subpublisher should be able to help you get this going much quicker than your accountant can because of much prior experience in these matters.

Subpublishers are usually empowered to issue full-rate mechanical licenses and to collect local performance income. The normal subpublishing agreement, though, requires approvals from the original publisher on all advertising, synchronizations, samples, and translations or adaptations within the territory. Rights not explicitly granted to a subpublisher should be reserved to the publisher. It is common that synchronization licenses, subject to the foregoing approval requirement, for films and programs originating and produced within the subpublisher's territory, may be issued for not just the local territory but for the world.

Finally, make sure you don't focus too much on the split of a proposed subpublishing deal and too little on the quality of the collections and reputation. A 10% commission with one company hardly ever results in the exact same net income to you as a 10% commission with a different company. And 75% of excellent collections is a lot more than 90% of poor collections. This point was brilliantly illustrated to me a few years ago when I switched from an 85%/15% deal with a multinational subpublisher covering South America, which had been producing a few hundred dollars' income per year, in favor of an 80%/20% deal with an independent that immediately paid out more than $10,000 on its first rendered royalty statements. There's always someone who will do it for less, but that doesn't mean you'll get more.

An Experiment Gone Wrong

Focusing on percentages instead of subjective qualities can also get a publisher into trouble in other ways. Many publishers have attempted to bypass subpublishers altogether and (where possible) collect directly from the foreign end music user, or directly from the foreign mechanical or performing right society. Since the local subpublisher is getting 10% of the money that he is getting from the local society, why not simply cut out that middleman and collect

10% more? In some territories for example, (MCPS in England, and NCB, or the Nordic Copyright Bureau, in Scandinavia), this practice is not prohibited by local law, and it is possible for a United States publisher to become a direct member.

I tried this some years ago in England (figuring there would be no language barrier) and obtained miserable results. The unfortunate xenophobic truth is that people give more attention and care to their own countrymen than they do to someone who doesn't know the local ropes and is separated by 6,000 miles and a ten-hour time difference. My conclusions were that paying a small sum for a subpublisher's local expertise is a good thing (penny wise vs. pound foolish) and that local law and custom are best dealt with by those operating in the territory and possessing the specific local knowledge and clout to get difficulties fixed, explained, or sorted out. Knowing how to work the local system and authorities (knowing who to bribe and when . . . just kidding!) is probably worth every cent you pay to an honest and hardworking subpublisher.

The Subpublisher Dinner Circuit

If you live in a major United States city and/or if your publishing catalog is significant enough, your subpublishers will most likely come to visit you every year or two. Recognizing the importance of maintaining personal relations while doing business at great distances, a very large number of subpublishers travel to the United States annually to meet and greet you or even to pitch you on their representation (if they don't work with you already). Face-to-face meetings with a great number of subpublishers in a short period of time are also possible at the MIDEM convention, held each January in Cannes, France. And if you are lucky enough to be able to travel to a subpublisher's city and country, you are likely to receive a warm welcome, fine hospitality, and accompanied local tours and sightseeing. One of my favorite aspects of the music publishing business is the genuine friendships that have developed with people in other countries and cultures, and the opportunity to travel to, know about, and feel comfortable in many areas of the world outside of the United States.

Cowriting and Copublishing

It is common practice now for more than one writer to collaborate on a song. If you review the writer credits for the songs on the Billboard "Hot 100" or "Hot R&B/Hip-Hop" charts, you will find many instances of four, five, or more writers and publishers on a given song. While some of these entities might be included due to incorporated samples, group collaboration is undoubtedly an important songwriting method these days.

It's important to understand how a song comes together and how publishers and their songwriters protect and legally handle the jointly created work. As we discussed previously, copyright exists once a song has been fixed in a tangible medium from which it may be reproduced. When there are two or more writers, in the absence of a written agreement to the contrary, copyright law deems that the split between the writers is equal, and makes no attempt to determine who contributed what and how important their contributions were. Except for nearly minimal contributions such as suggesting a title or changing a word or two or a note or two, each party is treated as the equal owner of an undivided interest in the song. When two writers collaborate, each owns a half of the whole song, even if one contributed only the lyrics and the other the music. When three writers collaborate, each one owns a third undivided interest. When four writers collaborate, each one owns a fourth undivided interest, and so on.

It is important for the writers to agree *when* the work is finished (when it has been fixed) because at this moment in time, several important concepts and rules kick in. If you and your cowriters are working on a song and you have to take a break for a few days, you all need to agree that the song isn't finished yet and is still a work in progress. Once the work is finished and has been recorded in some format, it becomes a *joint work* (which in copyright speak means that you have the intention that your "contributions be merged into inseparable or interdependent parts of a unitary whole"). From then on, further changes to the song have all sorts of ramifications and may even be prohibited by law if one of the writers does not want them. Such changes (to create a new song, version two, based on the first song) would constitute the creation of a derivative work, and if unauthorized might actually constitute copyright infringement. If this were not so, then your cowriter could effectively force you into collaborations and co-ownership situations with people you wouldn't want to collaborate with or perhaps had never met.

These rules lead to some possibly counterintuitive results. Let's look at a few examples.

If you collaborated on the lyrics with someone but wrote all the music, in the absence of a written agreement between the two of you to the contrary, each of you own half, even though you may feel as if you have done three-quarters of the work. There is no "separate but equal" concept with respect to music and words. As far as the copyright goes, you are equal creators of the joint work.

Here's another example. Let's say you finished a song with two cowriters, and then your cowriter, Bob, decides that the lyrics in the verse you wrote suck and wants to replace them with his own. Bob cannot do so without your permission, because that would constitute the creation of a derivative work based on the jointly completed, fixed copyright that had been created by the three of you. If you ultimately saw it Bob's way and agreed that your lyrics were actually bad and agreed to allow the removal of all of your contributions and lyrics in favor of new and improved ones by Bob, you could nonetheless lay claim to a one-third share of the new song, because you were a one-third owner of the finished song upon which the new work was based. This gives you the power, too, to prevent your contributions from being stripped out or altered from a finished work without your permission. Likewise, this prevents the dilution of your interest by the addition of more writers after you and your original cowriters have finished the song.

Obviously, fixing your finished work in a media (and thus stopping the clock on the creative process) could be an important step before you bring it into a recording session. Otherwise, the song could get "refinished" in a recording session or band rehearsal, and you could find yourself with four new claimants who decided or remembered that they helped you finish the song. Paranoia about this sort of thing can be bad for collaborations, but a laissez-faire attitude could also leave you with six cowriters. Bands working out songs together must have a clear internal understanding about the distinction between songwriting and simply working out bass and drum parts for your song. It is best to talk openly about this up front, and, if possible (I know, this is the music business), to collaborate only with those who you feel are aboveboard and honest.

Back to Reality

In reality, not everyone contributes equally. The copyright law's provisions are what take effect when you don't bother to decide among yourselves. It's kind of like dying without a will. When you don't make a will, the government will decide who gets what for you. If Joe the drummer only contributed a little bit to the song, you and Joe need to arrive at an agreement that his share was (for instance) only 20% and that your share was 80%. If you don't make this agreement, then the copyright goes automatically to the default 50%/50%. This type of agreement should be in writing but need not be complex or fancy to accomplish its basic intent. It might be written on a napkin or scrap of paper and say something as simple as, "On March 1, 2004, Joe D. Rummer and Bob DeGuitar finished a song called 'Whoo Hooo,' and the share of ownership is agreed to be 20% to Joe and 80% to Bob. [Signed Joe and Bob]." Sometimes the writing members of a group give a piece of the writer and/or publisher share to the nonwriting members just to keep them happy and to reward them for their other nonsongwriting efforts. Remember, though, that this is a gift and not an entitlement, so you should proceed carefully.

Don't Bogart That Joint (Work)

OK, so let's say that you are now the proud 25% co-owner of a fixed joint work and copyright. In short, you now co-own the music publishing on the song, and you need to know what you can do with it. In the absence of a written agreement by the other three writers (or their designated publishers) to the contrary, you are free to license the work on a *nonexclusive* basis without any permission from your cowriters or copublishers. While you legally have the right to grant nonexclusive licenses on behalf of 100% of the copyright, some potential licensers of the song will nonetheless insist upon obtaining licenses from your copublishers for their shares of the song.

What types of nonexclusive licenses can you grant without the other co-owners' permission? Provided that the song has already been publicly distributed, you can issue mechanical licenses for the whole song. (Since a first mechanical use can only happen once, it can be argued that a first mechanical use is an exclusive type of license.) Likewise, you can also grant nonexclusive synchronization licenses for the song to be used in TV shows, films, advertising, ringtones, sheet music, etc. The logic behind this provision of the law is that if one owner that has a chip on his shoulder or is in a feud with the other writers, he will not have the ability to prevent the others from enjoying the fruits of their labor by holding up the licensing.

Cowriters and copublishers issuing nonexclusive licenses on behalf of 100% of the song do nonetheless have obligations to the other writers and co-owners. They must take steps to ensure that crediting on these nonexclusive licenses includes all writers and publishers. They also have specific legal obligations including the obligation to account to the remaining writers (or publishers) for their rightful shares of the license fees.

Cowriters and copublishers do not have the right to issue exclusive licenses on behalf of the whole song. Such prohibitions include the exclusive right to use the song in advertising (where you explicitly agree that you will not license the song for any other advertisements during the license term), the exclusive right to print sheet music of the song, the exclusive right to subpublish the whole song (although you could grant your subpublisher the right to subpublish *your share* of the song), or the exclusive right to use the song as a television theme song. Any time you would like to issue a license that precludes your cowriters or copublishers from issuing a license to someone for the use of a song, it is *exclusive* in at least some aspect, and you (and the would-be licensee) thus require the consent of the copublishers. That also means your cowriters and copublishers can't issue an exclusive license without *your* consent, which protects your property as well.

Think about the ramifications of this. Your 10% copublisher cannot exclusively license 100% of the song to his uncle, the president of Coca-Cola, for $100, in all of Coke's worldwide advertisements. He could do it nonexclusively, but you would not then be precluded from approaching Pepsi-Cola and nonexclusively licensing 100% of the same song for Pepsi ads. It would be unlikely and even foolhardy for Coca-Cola to enter into a nonexclusive license to use the song in an advertising campaign that would cost millions of dollars if the company knew its rights were only nonexclusive and faced the possibility of someone else using the same theme song in other commercials. Practically and realistically speaking, the distinction between nonexclusive and exclusive licensing, and the rules about who can issue these licenses, protects all the parties well.

Finally, in the absence of a previously agreed prohibition, even though you do have the legal right to issue nonexclusive licenses on behalf of the whole song, it is not a very nice thing to do to your cowriter or copublisher. It is preferable, where possible and where all the writers are still speaking to one another, to discuss the terms and conditions of a proposed nonexclusive license, and to make the decisions mutually and in good faith. Licensing the whole song by yourself ought to be a last resort, like when your cowriter is in the Himalayas and forgot his cell phone and you'll lose the opportunity if you don't do it without him.

Even though potential licensees know that they could legally get a nonexclusive license from only you, they may not necessarily feel comfortable doing so. For example, what if they got a nonexclusive license from you to use the song on a TV show as a background vocal at a high school dance, and then your famous cowriter turned up and gave an interview to *Rolling Stone* where he talked about how much he hated that sitcom and how he never would have issued that license and what a rat you are? You can see why, where possible, licensers like to have all owners and writers on board. When they are desperate (the program airs in four hours and they have only gotten approval from one of the four publishers), they might go the less nice (but nonetheless legal) route.

Let's Make More Paper

When there is a reasonable likelihood that a collaboration will have significant exploitation, it is often advisable to have an agreement drawn up (a *co-administration agreement*) that specifies ownership, control (administration), and other important terms.

The most important function of a co-administration agreement is to list the writers and their percentages of the joint work. If the writers have assigned their works to publishing companies (even their own), the agreement lists the publishing companies and their respective shares as well along with all of the parties' respective addresses. The agreement provides for registration of the work in the U.S. Copyright Office according to the given terms and splits.

Administration of the joint work may be handled in several ways, and the chosen method is specified in the co-administration agreement. If one party is administering the whole song for the others (this would more likely be called a copublishing deal then), the agreement states that and lists and defines the obligations (accounting, obtaining approvals, clearing works with performing right societies, defending against infringements, etc.) that the administering party has to the other writers and publishers. More commonly, if all the parties are actually able to administer publishing rights, the agreement specifies that each party will directly administer, license, and collect their own respective shares only (including via their own respective subpublishers), and that each party is accepting an affirmative obligation to inform potential licensers that they must contact the copublishers to obtain licenses for the remaining shares.

In addition to normal contractual provisions such as venue and choice of law, cure periods, and breaches, co-administration agreements should also contemplate:

- The treatment of print rights (especially important if one or more of the writers already has a print deal).

- Controlled composition clauses (especially if one or more of the writers has or might have a record deal that subjects him to a controlled composition clause).

- Under which circumstances, if any, a reduced-rate mechanical license will be granted.

- The process for dealing with requests for derivative work licenses (samples, parodies, medleys, etc.).

- Promotional video rights in the event that one or more of the writers is also a recording artist who is likely to release promotional or concert videos.

- The accounting of inadvertently received moneys whereby one of the cowriters (or copublishers) receives all of the money for a given license and not his respective share.

- Warranties that each party's contribution to the joint work is original and noninfringing, along with related indemnifications.

- The defense of claims against one or more of the cowriters and copublishers with respect to the work, and the determination of when, if, and how to prosecute claims concerning the song against third parties.

- The sale of a party's respective interest, including possible matching or first-refusal rights.

Controlled
Composition Clauses

Controlled composition clauses, also referred to as "firstborn male child clauses" (at least as far as music publishers are concerned) are among the most detested parts of a typical recording artist agreement. Publishing mechanical royalties are usually paid from the first record distributed and are not usually subject to recoupment of any advances or recording costs. Because the license fees represent immediate out-of-pocket costs, the record companies like to do everything in their power to reduce and limit their amount and delay their payment.

A Controlled What?

The first part of any controlled composition clause is the definition of a *controlled composition*. Since the record company will eventually get around to asking for a reduced rate on controlled compositions, it behooves them to define what they are reducing as broadly as possible. Ideally they would like a controlled composition to be something like "any song you may have written or ever heard," and then they would like you to give them a discount on the mechanical rate to be charged for such song. Realistically, controlled compositions are more likely to be something like "any song written or cowritten by you, or any song owned, controlled, or administered by you." They will also endeavor to require that you agree that any musician, producer, engineer, arranger, etc. that you hire to work on your records also agrees to be bound by the terms of the clause. So not only do you have to get screwed, but you have to agree that you will require everyone else you work with to get screwed too.

If you are a recording artist and songwriter, and if you already have a publishing deal with a company, it is very important to ensure that a deal you are making with a record company does not conflict with the terms of the publishing deal and does not have you granting rights to the record company that are not yours to grant. Conversely, when making a publishing deal, it is important that the publishing company you are dealing with is aware of and accepts any controlled composition terms that you have agreed to in a recording agreement, which will result in a significant drop in income to the publisher.

The Meter Is Running

The first thing that enters into the controlled composition rate is the date upon which the reduced statutory rate will be based. In a perfect world you would receive a full statutory mechanical rate that "floats"—that is to say, a rate that is subject to future increases in the statutory rate. The first thing record companies want to do is stop the clock. Actually, they want to *turn it back*. Specifically, what they try to do is fix the mechanical rate basis even before the date the record is released and maybe even before the song was written. The wording in the controlled composition clause thus states something like the mechanical rate is based on "the earlier of the date that you turn in the record, or the date that you were contractually required to turn in the record." The idea is that they would like to pay you based on the statutory rate that was in effect before its last increase and even before the date your record was released.

Since United States mechanical rates change every two years, the chances are at least 50/50 that you are less than a year away from a statutory rate change at any given time. Delayed releases are extremely common due to remixing, recording of additional songs, availability in release schedules, additional up-front time required to set up the initial release (preparing videos, ad campaigns, etc.), and coordination with live performance tours. So there can be a long (or at least longer than you'd probably like) lag between the time you turn in the record and when it actually comes out. Further, since the label reps pick an arbitrary due date upon which you are required to turn in the record, they argue that just because they were nice enough to let you turn in your record late, why should they suffer and pay a higher mechanical rate than they would have if you had it delivered on time? If possible, you should try to have the controlled composition mechanical rate be the one in effect on the date of release.

Our Special Reducing Formula

The next thing that a controlled composition clause does is to reduce the rate that will be paid in as many ways as possible. The record company tries to have a clause with wording that says you will (typically) get a "mechanical rate based on 75% of the fixed minimum statutory rate." As discussed above, the label will also try to take steps to ensure that the statutory rate it is paying you 75% of is last year's model. Two words, here, *fixed* and *minimum*, will also prevent you from enjoying eventual increases in the statutory rate and from enjoying any long-song payments.

Since record company greed, like most other forms of corporate greed, knows no bounds, the controlled composition clause will also try for further reductions in the rate by giving it a definitional name such as "Your Mechanical Rate" and then proceeding to list various circumstances and types of additional reductions that can be taken with respect to Your Mechanical Rate.

For instance, the label will try to obtain rate reductions for lower price configurations. Perhaps, "mid-line" units (i.e., those sold for less than top-line, full-priced releases) and "record club" units might be paid at 75% of Your Mechanical Rate, and "budget" releases at 50% of Your Mechanical Rate. So you are now looking at 75% of 75%, or even 50% of 75% of the fixed minimum outdated mechanical rate. Labels will also attempt to specify that they are only required to pay these mechanical rates "on royalty-bearing units." Elsewhere in the agreement, "royalty bearing units" will be defined to exclude things like "free goods" (discussed in the mechanical royalty chapter), "special free goods," "promotional copies," and anything else they might be able to think of. So with

15% taken out, they will now be paying you 85% of Your Mechanical Rate, again with configuration reductions (where applicable) discussed above. Are you sick yet?

The types of reductions record companies think of seem boundless. Because the controlled composition clause might read to the effect that "you hereby license 'controlled compositions' to us for use on phonorecords" at the specified rates and terms, you are not just licensing your shares of these songs, but all of your cowriters' shares as well. Because of this "you are hereby licensing" wording, they will also take the position that the recording agreement constitutes a license in and of itself, and they don't need another piece of paper to explicitly license any of the controlled compositions to them. This means that they are effectively calculating the rate themselves, and that because you or your representative is not issuing a specific license to them, you often will not know (let alone agree with) what rate they are paying until they've begun accounting to you. Lastly, because you are licensing the controlled compositions to them "for use on phonorecords" *as opposed to for use on specifically identified phonorecords*, they may even get the opportunity to turn the clock back further in the future. When you release a live album, a best-of album, or a greatest hits album, you may well find that they have the right (according to the controlled composition clause) to pay you for the use of the controlled compositions not at the rate in effect at the time of the new release, but at the rate in effect for when you first "hereby licensed" the song to them eight years ago.

Just in Case That Isn't Enough

In order to ensure that you aren't as sneaky as they are, record companies have also introduced the concept of an *aggregate mechanical cap*. What would happen to the record companies if recording artists actually wanted to give record buyers more value by putting, say, 15 songs on a CD? Well, they'd have to pay mechanical royalties on these songs. Or, heaven forbid, what if an artist turned in a record that had 30 two-minute songs on it? To guard against this possibility, the record companies have come up with an aggregate mechanical cap that typically runs from ten times Your Mechanical Rate for baby bands to 14 times Your Mechanical Rate for superstar acts.

To see how this works, let's say you're in a mid-level band and you have a 12-song cap. So you multiply Your Mechanical Rate (which may already be hugely reduced, as discussed above) by 12, and that is all the money that the record company is obligated to pay you for mechanical royalties. But you have 14 great songs and you want to put all of them on your record. Penalty time! Since you have already agreed that the label has to pay you at most 12 times Your Mechanical Rate, and since your maximum mechanical rate pool only covers 12 songs, you have now effectively agreed to a further 2/14ths reduction of Your Mechanical Rate. Ha ha! You lose!

But there's more. Let's say that you didn't write all of the songs on the record. Let's say you've done a cover recording of Bob Dylan's "Lay Lady Lay," plus another song you were lucky enough to cowrite with Mick Jagger, and a third song you wrote with your brother-in-law who isn't in your group and isn't subject to your recording agreement. Dylan's music publishers, although they are very nice, don't see why they should accept your controlled composition rate (they get no benefit from your recording agreement, after all) and regretfully insist upon a full floating long-song statutory rate on all units made and distributed. Mick Jagger, too, figures that he is entitled to a full rate for his half of the song, even if you have agreed to accept Your Mechanical Rate for your half of the song. Your brother-in-law, though, is someone whom you can browbeat to share the suffering. (He no doubt deserves it and you'd enjoy it. Why should he make more for his half of the song than you make for your half of the song? So go ahead!)

So before any mechanical rates can be calculated for the songs on the record, you have to reduce your allocable mechanical rate pool by the full current long-song (where applicable) statutory rate times $1^1/_2$ songs to pay Dylan and Jagger. Then you get to allocate the remaining money, which for argument's sake let's say amounts to $10^1/_2$ times Your Mechanical Rate (it may be less because Dylan and Jagger might be paid at the long-song current statutory rate, and your aggregate mechanical cap might be based on an older noncurrent rate). You now take this $10^{1}/_{2}$ times Your Mechanical Rate pool and you allocate it over the $12^{1}/_{2}$ songs written by you and your controlled brother-in-law (i.e., 14 songs total less Dylan's song less Jagger's half song), and you are thus left with each of your songs getting $10^{1}/_{2}/12^{1}/_{2}$ of Your Mechanical Rate, which is worse even than the 12/14 reduction of two paragraphs ago. (Dylan and Jagger are used only hypothetically here, and their respective publishers may have different positions and reactions than we've attributed to them in this illustration. Or they may not.)

Since you've "hereby licensed" the whole song, you have to be particularly cautious about the treatment of your cowriters. If they don't agree to be "controlled" (i.e., to go along with your controlled composition rate, terms, and payment methodology) and insist upon a full rate, that amount will come out of your aggregate mechanical pool, making you in effect pay the differential between your cowriter's share of a full floating long-song statutory rate and your cowriter's share of Your Mechanical Rate, thus even further reducing the mechanical pool allocable to your songs (and your brother-in-law's too).

Some controlled composition clauses are kind enough to anticipate that there might be a few "outside" songs, and may have a separate mechanical pool allowance for payment of full floating statutory payments for such songs that does not affect or reduce the artist's own aggregate mechanical cap or pool. Additionally, some recording artists with sufficient clout or with a proclivity toward putting out albums that contain fewer but longer songs have been able to get *min-max* wording put into their controlled composition clauses. These clauses, while limiting the worst-case scenario to the record company (the maximum aggregate cap) conversely protect the songwriting recording artist. If such an artist has a "12 times min-max" clause but turns in an album that has ten lengthy songs on it, the proration would be reversed and might allow the artist to receive 12/10ths of Your Mechanical Rate, sometimes resulting in a greater than statutory mechanical payment. You see these min-max clauses more often in older recording agreements under which vinyl records were the primary sound-carrying media, with their limited number of songs and playing time relative to CDs.

Recording artists who write little or none of their own material might require different sorts of controlled composition clauses. Such recording agreements may even provide that the record company (perhaps jointly with the artist) gets to pick and approve the proposed song list and number of songs, and is responsible for obtaining mechanical licenses at the best rates it can, and for its own sole benefit, for all of the "outside" songs (i.e., noncontrolled compositions).

Et Tu, Brute?

Controlled composition clauses also tend to provide for reduced-rate mechanicals in Canada. (Outside of the United States and Canada, mechanical rates are rarely, if ever, reduced, and most recording agreements specify that the rates payable outside of the United States and Canada will be paid according to local rate and custom.) Many of the Canadian reductions parallel the reductions of the United States rate. Because Canada has eliminated its statutory rate, the controlled composition reductions are typically based on the "usual and customary" Canadian rate, or the rate specified under the CRIA-CMRRA schemes discussed in the mechanical licensing chapter.

The CRIA-CMRRA schemes have also been known to include terms that the members of CRIA have agreed will supercede lower rates or smaller aggregate caps specified in a particular recording agreement. So it is advisable to check on these terms when issuing mechanical licenses for controlled artists in Canada. By virtue of the whole-industry agreement, you might actually be entitled to a better rate than you agreed to, but only if you know about it and ask for it.

Wait, There's More!

Modern controlled composition clauses have even broadened the applicability beyond mechanical uses. The clauses will likely have provisions giving the record company the right to have a free synchronization license for a controlled composition if it produces a promotional music video. There might also be a "just in case" clause specifying that if you ever release a live concert home videotape or DVD, you have agreed up front to what the rates on that hypothetical product will be. Record companies would like you to agree to this now, when the products are only pie in the sky and you are less likely to negotiate hard for the proper or fair rate.

New technologies such as ringtones and DPD deliveries are finding their ways into controlled composition wording, and again, even though such uses may not be presently contemplated, it is important to take proper care to ensure that you won't regret what you agree to now sometime down the road.

Seen It All Before? Or Have You?

When writing this chapter, I did not once look at a controlled composition clause; instead I relied solely on past history and experience with hundreds of such clauses. The intention was to avoid picking on any one record company's clause, or to point out any specifically onerous points incorporated by any particular company. Controlled composition wording is continually evolving or devolving (depending upon whether you're on the record company or music publisher side of the fence). There is always someone somewhere thinking of new, exciting, and not readily apparent ways to pay less money to music publishers and to (believe it or not) downplay the importance and value of songs in the music business.

Can You Make It All Go Away?

You can get a de facto admission from most of the major record companies that what they are doing with controlled composition clauses is over the top if you accept their offer to make a publishing deal with their sister music publisher. Almost all major record companies possess music publishing divisions, and if you agree to make a deal with them, many record companies will agree to much more favorable terms (to you) in your controlled composition clause. To use a hackneyed phrase, this deal may be like taking from Peter to pay Paul, or like hiring the fox to guard the henhouse. The typical trade-off in such an arrangement would be to base Your

Mechanical Rate on a full statutory mechanical rate, possibly even floating and not fixed at a point in time, in exchange for making a copublishing agreement where you give the sister publishing company ownership of half of your publisher's share. Since half of the publisher's share is really only 50% of 50%, or 25% of the whole, the argument goes that by giving up 25% of the ownership, you are getting an extra 25% on your mechanical rate. And that means, the argument might continue, that while the proposed copublishing agreement only goes for a period of years (maybe 12?), the benefit that you obtain in terms of getting a full rate will go on forever, or for as long as the company continues to sell your records.

In analyzing these proposals, you should evaluate how deeply you want to get into business with one particular company. While synergy may be the watchword of the day, in this case it may just mean giving up more rights and shortchanging your own best interests. You should examine if you want one sole company to control both your master and publishing rights, or whether you want separate controls, checks, and balances. Remember, too, that if you become very successful as an artist and songwriter, you will have the clout to renegotiate your deals and terms, especially your artist royalty and mechanical rates. Record companies always want more records from successful artists and feel the very real necessity and benefit of keeping them happy. The clout that comes from past success (or from perceived market competition for a given recording artist's or songwriter's services) may well allow better terms in the initial or renegotiated agreement.

More On Copyright

In the "Overview" we covered some of the fundamental terms and concepts of music copyright law. This chapter takes a more detailed survey of the copyright issues that are most relevant to songwriters and music publishers. For further depth or research, the United States Copyright Office provides much good information online (www.copyright.gov), including information circulars, text of laws and regulations, and even downloadable blank and fill-in PDF forms. There are also many good books and periodicals on various aspects of this field covering a wide variety of specific topics and issues. An attorney well versed in copyright law can be invaluable for evaluating and resolving specific situations. Unless specifically mentioned to the contrary, this discussion relates only to songs written after January 1, 1978, the effective date of the 1976 Copyright Act.

As discussed previously, your ownership of the copyright in your song exists automatically once you have fixed it in a copy or phonorecord. Nonetheless, there are advantages to making your claim a matter of public record promptly after creation, and you are precluded from bringing an infringement suit until you have made such a registration.

Hey PA, What's This Form?

The PA form is used to register works of the performing arts. This includes songs consisting of words and music, or just music. There are two forms of registration, in either unpublished form (indicated by a registration number beginning with PAu) or published form (indicated by a registration number beginning with PA). Both afford you many of the same protections; the main difference is that a PAu registration protects the work even if you have not yet distributed copies or phonorecords to the general public. In some instances, a song may be copyrighted first as an unpublished work and subsequently as a published work. One advantage to first copyrighting a song in unpublished form is that you are demonstrating the song is "finished," and thus any subsequent modifications or additions constitute derivative works.

Let's say you send your song out to a recording artist to consider for her next album, and you have already submitted a PA copyright registration in unpublished form. If she, at a later date and without telling you, writes two more verses and reworks your bridge, puts it on her album, and claims half the writing and publishing credits, you can certainly cut her off at the pass. (Of course, it would be a different story if she came to you up front and got your permission and blessing to do so.)

The current cost for a PA or PAu registration is $30. Additionally, along with your payment and filled out form, you have to submit a nonreturnable copy of your work (referred to as the deposit) in the "best edition." According to the Copyright Office, the best edition is the "one of the highest quality" and fullest available recorded demonstration of the song. Your deposit may be a CD, vinyl disc, tape, written sheet music, etc. If you want to get more bang for your limited buck, you can submit a single $30 PA form covering a number of songs as a collection of musical works, in either unpublished or published form. A condition of this collective registration is that all the songs have to have the same owner and same authorship. One song cannot be written, owned, and claimed by your bass player while another is written, owned, and claimed by your lead guitar player. But if you have 12 songs written by you and Mr. Lead Guitar Player together, and if you jointly own all of these songs, you can register these songs and spend $30 only once instead of 12 times. In published form, the requirement for common authorship in collections of works is waived, but the common ownership requirement remains.

Anyone can register a work in unpublished form, regardless of home base or nationality. For published registrations, there are restrictions, but registration is allowed if one of the writers is living in the United States or is a citizen, or if the first commercial release is in the U.S. The date of registration is the date that the Copyright Office receives the whole package from you in acceptable form. It may nonetheless take six months or more to get the completed form back from the Copyright Office, especially if there is an anthrax scare and everything sits untouched in a room at the Copyright Office for six months. The duration of copyright runs the author's entire life plus 70 years thereafter. If you are drug-addled loser and die when you're 28, but your songwriting partner is Mr. Healthy, the 70 years doesn't start running until he dies. Good advice is to write with people who are more talented and healthier than you are.

A mention must be made here, too, of an embarrassing problem that the Copyright Office is currently experiencing. Many music publishers are finding that the Copyright Office claims to have received the application and payment but not the deposit that was sent. Copyright Office employees have admitted to me that there is a theft problem within their ranks. If you send in a nice new CD for registration, someone might just walk off with it and you might be asked to send another one. Likewise, if you send in a tape of unreleased demo songs by a superstar artist, you better hope they don't end up on Ebay. It is incredibly frustrating that the parties charged with protecting your works might be stealing or bootlegging them. Always save a copy of what you are sending as a deposit. Additionally, it is unfortunately advisable that you send your whole package by a traceable method of delivery (certified mail, FedEx, etc.). If this problem doesn't get any better, you can do what I do and submit the copyright registration to the specific honest examiner known to me, after letting him/her know by phone or fax that the registration is on the way.

Wait, I Changed My Mind

Let's say you have sold, given, or otherwise transferred your copyrights (registered after January 1, 1978) to another party at some point in your career. This could be anyone from a music publisher to your brother-in-law, your ex-wife, or a tax trust. You have a legal right to terminate that transfer of your copyrights even if it completely contradicts a written transfer agreement. This termination right comes 35 years after the date of the written transfer. So the first possible effective termination date for copyrights registered on January 1, 1978, would be in the year 2013. There are very specific regulations as to how you serve notice that you are terminating your transfer and taking your copyrights back. The timing of this notice has to be at least two years but not more than ten years prior to the effective termination date. So we are just now seeing authors beginning to serve termination notices that will be effective in 2013.

There are some murky issues in all of this that are going to have to be resolved. For example, the termination provisions of the law make reference to transfers executed after January 1, 1978. But what if someone signed on January 1, 1977, a three-year publishing deal that transferred everything that she wrote for the next three years? Were the works written in 1978 and 1979, even though their creation and transfer were contemplated in 1977, nonetheless transferred before their creation, thus robbing the author of the right to terminate the transfer? Or would a court hold that a transfer of ownership cannot take place until the works' creation and existence?

For older works written on or prior to December 31, 1977, the authors of such works have two five-year windows in which to terminate the transfer: either the five years prior to 56 years after the initial registration, or the five years prior to 75 years after the initial registration.

Such terminations are effective in the United States only, and do not afford you the right to recover your songs outside of the United States. Additionally, licenses issued by the party from which you have recovered your rights (or will recover your rights) may still be binding upon you, even if the term of that license has run past the date of the effective termination. You should know, too, that transfers cannot be terminated if they are part of someone's will. So if Dad always liked you better and gave you his songs on his deathbed, your sister, as the trustee of his estate, can't terminate that transfer and get the songs away from you. The bottom line is that terminations are a gift from the government, and anything you can get back is better than everything that you gave away.

The Corporation Wrote Your Song

A work-for-hire song is written under a person's scope of employment. The results and proceeds of that work (including the right to claim authorship and ownership) do not reside with the "employee for hire" but rather with the "employer for hire." Without getting too technical, an example is if someone hires you on a work-for-hire basis to write a jingle or to score a movie. The ad agency or the studio, in these cases, is the legal author of the music and the legal owner. Unless your agreement with the ad agency or studio provides for additional compensation or royalties, your fee is your complete consideration. Work-for-hire copyright duration is the shorter of 120 years from creation or 95 years from first publication. It should be noted, too, that works-for-hire are not subject to terminations of transfer, so think really hard about what you're doing when you agree to work for hire.

I Feel Renewed

Songs created prior to January 1, 1978, are subject to older copyright laws and have an initial 28-year term, a 28-year renewal term, and then two additional terms (added by new laws) of 19 and 20 years respectively, for a total possible duration of 95 years. Copyrights expire at the end of the appropriate year, not on the anniversary of the registration date. Renewals of copyrights are filed on an RE form and must be done in the author's name. The cost is $60.

Transfers and Other Forms

The Copyright Office maintains a transfer registry. Since all copyright is initially vested to the author, and since all copyright transfers are required to be in writing (you can't just tell your manager, "Here, I'm giving this song to you," thank God), the Copyright Office must reflect a transfer if the author is not the final or eventual claimant. A transfer may be indicated on the original PA registration where you are asked to check a box explaining how you arrived at being the registered claimant ("by written assignment" is sufficient where accurate). If a transfer of ownership occurs after the initial registration has been made, the transfer documents can be recorded in the Copyright Office transfer registry as public notice that the ownership has changed. Other documents relating to ownership, liens, etc. may also be recorded in the transfer registry. The cost is $80 for the recordation of a document with one title, with $20 additional per extra song title up to ten.

A CA form can be filed to correct errors in previous registrations. The cost is $100. The Copyright Office is pretty happy to take your money for just about anything you can reasonably think of as well. For example, if you don't want to wait six months to get your form back, you can expedite the registration for $580. If you can't find a registration you are looking for, the Copyright Office charges $80 per hour to research it for you. If you'd like an extra copy of your certificate, the cost is $30. Aside from the thieves in their midst, the Copyright Office workers are generally a helpful and accommodating bunch.

Can You Help Me, SR?

Another way of registering a song is as part of a sound recording (SR copyright) registration. This can be done only in limited circumstances where the ownership of the copyrights in the sound recording and in the musical composition is exactly the same. The authorship statement in section 2 of the SR form should state that you are claiming both works. So if you and your band intend to jointly own the master recording but you are the sole songwriting claimant, this type of registration would not work for you.

The Advantages of Being Dead

If you are dead, you can't be held to performance of a written songwriting agreement after your death. This good news means that if you assigned someone a copyright and renewal rights, but then you went ahead and died before the renewal rights accrued to you, the renewal rights were thus not transferable by you. In practical terms, this means that if you died before the date that a copyright was eligible to be renewed (this is only applicable for a pre-1978 copyright), your assignee doesn't get to claim United States renewal rights—your heirs do. Now aren't you glad you died?

This benefit is different than terminating a transfer because you have to be dead to enjoy it. Make sure your heirs know that they have or might have this right, so they don't get bamboozled into reassigning the renewal right to the original publisher. If you're only near death, but some of your works will be eligible for renewal in the future, you should explain to your heirs how all this works. With respect to a 1978 and post copyright, the right to terminate after 35 years again resides with your heirs, but since there is no renewal on 1978 and post copyrights (remember, you get "the author's life plus 70 years" on these), there is no renewal right for the heirs to claim.

As we discussed earlier in this chapter in the "Wait, I Changed My Mind" section, being dead only benefits your heirs in the United States. Other copyright laws in other countries (such as the United Kingdom) may recognize the concept of reversionary interests. In order to maximize the benefit of your death in this regard, it would be advisable to seek out legal counsel well versed in international copyright laws.

The Advantages of Being Foreign

Finally, please remember that the subject matter discussed has been oriented primarily to music publishing within the United States. Other countries have different copyright laws and customs, some of which are remarkably similar to ours and others of which are significantly different. There have been many international treaties seeking to standardize copyright protections from one country to another, and to ensure reciprocal protections of copyright to citizens of countries signatory to such treaties. Such treaties include the U.C.C. (Universal Copyright Convention, 1954) and the Berne Convention for the Protection of Literary and Artistic Works (1989).

The Berne Convention significantly includes the concept of an author's *moral rights*, which says, "Independently of the author's economic rights, and even after the transfer of the said rights, the author shall have the right to claim authorship of the work and to object to any distortion, mutilation, or other modification of, or other derogatory action in relation to, the said work, which would be prejudicial to his honor or reputation." Sadly, the United States has not amended its copyright laws to comply with this internationally recognized protection for creators, while nonetheless maintaining that it otherwise adheres to the Berne Convention. Some have speculated that this situation is due to lobbying by the United States' film industry, which desires to maintain the broadest possible rights in work-for-hire productions without any regard for rights that are "morally" (if not via ownership) possessed by the creators.

Representation and Further Advice

This chapter will cover a variety of loosely related topics that warrant some discussion but are not significant enough to justify complete chapters in their own right. Consider this the free advice section.

You Get What You Pay For

It is often the case that newer songwriters and publishers cannot afford proper representation when entering into new agreements. It is also often the case that established songwriters and publishers don't *want* to afford proper representation. In many cases this leads to negative long-term consequences.

When hiring a lawyer, be sure to choose someone with significant prior experience in the areas that you need. Just because some guy has graduated from law school and passed the bar exam doesn't necessarily mean he knows the first thing about recording or publishing agreements, or that he has any real-world experience that will allow him advise you about what is normal what is not. Your cousin Vinny might be a lawyer and willing to cut you a great deal, but he might not know the first thing about a controlled composition clause. Sure, he'll look it up in some books and articles and do the research, but someone who deals with these issues day in, day out, will be much more effective.

It is also likely that more experienced counsel, although costing much more per hour, will be able to finish the job in much less time. It is possible, even, that such counsel has previously negotiated with that same company and same agreement form and can get to the end much more quickly and cheaply by just saying, "Hey, can you just incorporate the changes we made in the Joe Blow deal into this one?" While each agreement is different and each client has different needs, someone with experience can get to your specifics more efficiently.

Inexperienced attorneys are (in my experience) more likely to heavily mark up an agreement to demonstrate to their clients the value of the services. Unless the client is an attorney himself, or unless he possesses genuine knowledge and industry experience, the marked-up agreement is likely to seem impressive. On the other hand, a plethora of ridiculous or inappropriate comments telegraphs to the other side that the attorney does not know what he is doing and does not understand industry norms.

Another point to consider, too, is that experience is real and tangible but clout is only perceived. If a record or publishing company is offering you a great deal, it is because *you* are that valuable. It is not because your lawyer is some big kahuna that the company reps are shocked and awed by. While Mr. Kahuna might be able to get them on the phone quicker, and might be able to call in some favors or a tit-for-tat to push over a given point, the basic value of the deal accrues to you and your talent. A bombastic lawyer or manager who brags that he got you an $8 million deal did so because the company wanted you that badly, and it would have given the same deal, more or less, to anyone else who could offer your services. Don't forget that the worth of your own services is what ultimately drives any music deal.

Some attorneys and business managers like to or are willing to work on a percentage basis instead of an hourly (or by the job) basis. Typically, this percentage is around 5%. (Correspondingly, almost all personal managers work on a percentage basis.) It is therefore very important to consider how the method of compensation is likely to color a negotiation. Attorneys and managers who are receiving a percentage of your deal may feel an incentive to front-load the deal with cash as opposed to maximizing long-term benefit and revenue. These people may not be secure in the knowledge that you will want them to represent you for the long haul, and they may simply want to get decent compensation for their work now. This dynamic may lead to deals in which the up-front guarantees are strengthened at the expense of a lower and more disadvantageous split of income to you or a longer agreement term.

It would certainly be an uncomfortable situation if, deep into a negotiation, you start wondering whether the advice and representation you are getting is untainted. While tainting is a possibility in this percentage scenario, it is also possible to receive questionable advice on an hourly basis. There is not a week that goes by when I do not see the flames of what would seem to be an easily resolved dispute fanned and made worse because someone keeps getting $400 per hour as long as the dispute is not resolved. In fact, if lawyers' hourly rates went down retroactively the longer a dispute went on, you'd see things settled and resolved much quicker.

It is also possible to put a cap on a fee for a given job ("You'll do this job for $400 an hour, but in any event you won't charge me more than $10,000"). This can limit your costs, but it can also serve to limit the amount of attention the deal gets if it runs into unforeseen problems.

So where does this leave you? It is certainly hard when you distrust parties who are supposed to have your best interests in mind. Keep your eyes open and beware of pitfalls. If something doesn't seem right, get a second opinion.

My Lawyer Is a Sewer, er, Suer

In the music business, there are generally two types of attorneys, transactional attorneys and litigation attorneys. In some cases, but not often, attorneys do both transactional work and litigation work.

Transactional attorneys specialize in negotiating deals and handling day-to-day commerce. For example, they might negotiate publishing and record deals, set up and maintain corporation and partnership agreements, help you negotiate deals with band members or cowriters, and work with publishing administrators on music licenses.

Litigation counsel specializes in filing and handling lawsuits and defending against them. As examples, litigation attorneys might defend against a suit in which someone claims that your song was stolen from theirs. Or these attorneys might sue the record company for failing to account to you properly. Litigation in the United States tends to be very, very expensive and the costs (which are likely to be higher than you could imagine or project) should be carefully weighed against the potential benefits, financial or otherwise. Going to court to right a wrong or for egotistical reasons (be honest with yourself) is a luxury to be accorded only the wealthiest individuals or large corporations.

If, however, there is a genuine dispute involving more money or significance than the legal fees are likely to cost, and if you know you would be willing to take the matter to court, it is probably worthwhile to immediately retain litigation counsel and not have a transactional counsel as the lead player. The attorneys and players on the other side may, unfortunately, be dismissive of what they face when contacted by a transactional attorney. They know they are fairly free from litigation costs or any real danger until you have hired a litigator. They know that if they can't get the matter resolved with your transactional attorney, they get one more chance at settlement with the litigator you will then have to hire. In other words, they may not fear or respect a lawyer they know won't sue them. Although transactional attorneys often work for firms that also have litigation attorneys, in order for your position to be taken seriously, it may be unfortunately necessary to bring in the litigators. Sometimes you get more with a big stick; sometimes you don't.

A Boy Named Sue

Inevitably, and way too frequently when you have a hit song, you yourself will be sued. As soon as that money starts landing in your account, people come out of the woodwork claiming that they wrote your song and you stole it, nyeah nyeah nyeah. On a recent hit song administered by my company, I had three unrelated parties come out and say that the song was written by them and stolen. My suggestion that there be an elimination tournament, whereby the three potential claimants would fight it out for the right to sue my client in a Super Suit, was not met with favorably.

Almost all of these suits are nuisances, often brought maliciously, and often banking on fears of bad publicity. Unfortunately, the saying that "every suit has a nuisance settlement value" is often true. You are often stuck with the unsatisfying choice of paying someone $20,000 to go away (without admitting any guilt) versus spending $200,000 in litigation defense costs that you might never recover even if you prevail.

In infringement suits, the plaintiff must prove both that you had access to his material and also that a substantial similarity to the allegedly infringed work exists. To eliminate the access claim, it is highly advisable not to listen to or even accept any unsolicited tapes or songs from anyone you don't know or have any doubts about. Nonetheless, access to the allegedly infringed work can be claimed or proven if the original work was publicly disseminated (for example, if it was on a well-known record or played on the radio millions of times). "Substantial similarity" will be argued by the musicologists on both sides, but in reality, both judges and juries will listen to the two works in question and make up their own minds regardless of what the experts have to say.

Let Us Count This Day Our Daily Beans

At a certain level, you may want to switch from your local family accountant to a business manager. Business managers offer all the same tax and bookkeeping services that your local accountant does, but they augment it with (you hope) keener business advice, tax planning and structuring, and investment knowledge. They also handle many of the day-to-day aspects of insurance acquisition, bill paying, home and automobile purchases, etc. In any case where clients have significant income, it is important not to blindly abdicate responsibility for money and investments to a third party. Take reasonable care in selecting a business manager, and be sure to maintain oversight and awareness of your situation no matter how boring or technical it may be.

The music business is filled with people who made millions of dollars on one hit in the '60s or '70s but now struggle to get by on what little income oldies tours or their name can get them because they blew it all on drugs, houses, divorces, and private jets. Likewise, there are people who had that same one hit but are comfortably living out their years in a paid-for house in Bel Air, using those modest royalty payments to pay the property taxes and put their kids through college.

A couple of specific bits of advice:

- Know how much money and other assets you have and where they are, and be comfortable in the understanding that everything is in your name.

- Be very wary of investing in businesses with your manager, attorney, or business manager. You want them as noninterested advisors, not as your partners.

- If your investment involves offshore partnerships and trusts, and complicated tax strategies that you don't remotely understand, make sure that you also have significant investments and assets that could support you if the complicated stuff disappears. While some complicated tax and asset management strategies are brilliant, others are simply complicated and may even be disallowed.

- Sign your own checks, and review your own monthly statements. There is no other way to know what you are spending or what you have.

Know What They Owe

Auditing a record company or a publishing company is one of the smartest things a recording artist or songwriter can do. Most recording and publishing contracts are written so as to limit any potential liability to the company to the amount of recovery. In other words, there is often no specified penalty or interest owed to you when you discover how much you have not been paid. The typical worst-case scenario for a record or publishing company is that they get forced to pay you the money they already were bound to pay you in the first place. While there are penalties and civil remedies available extra-contractually for fraud, most of the errors made in the company's favor are characterized as "inadvertent," "unintentional," or "subject to contractual interpretation." But then again, most of the errors do seem to be in the companies' favor, so maybe they really are just convenient mistakes?

Anyone with earnings of more than a few hundred thousand dollars over a three-year period is advised to audit a record company. Record company accounting is extremely complex and even convoluted. I have almost never seen a record company audit that did not recover at least the auditor's costs, and for this reason, it is often possible to find competent and qualified auditors willing to work on a contingent fee basis. An artist who has released four to six albums auditing a major record company over the last three years' statements (typically the contractual limit) might expect to spend $25,000 to $45,000 for such an audit, depending on the specifics. A new artist auditing only one or two albums would spend less, and an established artist with 27 albums, and four different record company accounts, obviously significantly more.

The publishing threshold for when an audit is justifiable might be higher than for record companies because publishers generally do not manufacture and distribute physical products. In fact, in the absence of fraud or intentional malfeasance, most publishing companies do a fairly good job of passing on your share of the receipts and accounting to you. Many of the potential payment shortfalls found in a publishing audit may even be apparent from the statements themselves. For example, if the publisher is supposed to pay you 75% of the income but is only paying you 67.5%, you can see that you have a problem without going in for an audit. Publishing company audits generally reveal claims of the nature of income that the company should have collected but didn't (i.e., poor publishing administration results in unregistered and uncollected income), or upstream commission or tax deductions that are not contractually permissible. For these reasons, it is much harder to make a publishing company audit pay off than a record company audit.

You should not worry about offending your record or publishing company by auditing them. While they hope you won't, auditing is a normal part of everyday business that they expect to deal with. Even if your account is unrecouped due to advances, an audit is advisable if there is a chance that your account might someday recoup. The proceeds of the audit, when applied to an unrecouped balance, bring you that much closer to payable balances.

Learn Me More

The topics covered in this book comprise a survey of most of the important things you will need to know on a day-to-day basis. In fact, if you understand and absorb most of the content, you'll be ahead of 90% of the pack.

When things get complicated beyond the scope of the basic information presented here, there are several good places and ways to get more information, and there are people (international copyright attorneys, for example) who specialize in very specific and limited aspects of copyright and music publishing fields. As noted elsewhere, excellent information is available online through the United States Copyright Office (www.copyright.gov).

There are many good books on music publishing, and specialized aspects of music publishing, such as *Nimmer On Copyright* by Melville B. Nimmer and David Nimmer (Matthew Bender) and *Kohn On Music Licensing* by Al Kohn and Bob Kohn (Aspen Publishers).

Appendix:
Can You Do the Splits?

The process of splitting publishing money is often very confusing, especially because the splits for performing income and other types of income are not the same. For example, a writer might receive 45% of a publisher's performing right receipts and 67.5% of a publisher's mechanical right receipts.

To help you understand how splits typically work, here are a series of common scenarios that get progressively more complex. For novices (and even non-novices), it is often useful to make diagrams with summaries at the end, as I have done here. These examples show the ultimate disposition of $100 in earnings, but can also be viewed as showing how 100% of income is split.

1. John is a 100% writer and Stinky Songs is the 100% publisher.

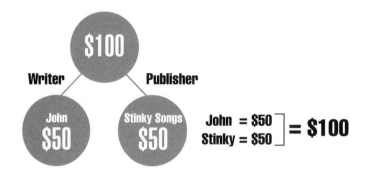

Summary

Performance income:

Performing right society pays $50 to John as writer share.

Performing right society pays $50 to Stinky as publisher share.

Other income:

Source pays Stinky $100. Stinky pays John $50, or 50%, as writer share.

Thus Stinky pays none of its performing right receipts to John, and 50% of all other receipts to him.

2. John and Bill are each 50% writers and Stinky Songs is the 100% publisher.

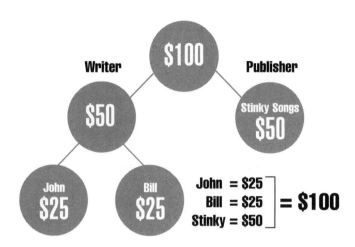

Summary
Performance income:

Performing right society pays $25 to John as writer share and $25 to Bill as writer share.

Performing right society pays $50 to Stinky as publisher share.

Other income:

Source pays Stinky $100. Stinky pays $25 (25/100, or 25%) each to John and Bill as writer shares. Stinky retains $50, or 50%.

Thus Stinky pays none of its performing right receipts to any writer, and 25% of other receipts to John and 25% to Bill.

3. **John is the sole writer and has a 50%/50% copublishing deal with Stinky Songs.**

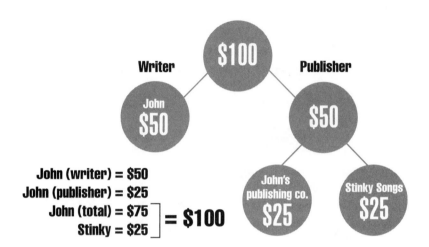

John (writer) = $50
John (publisher) = $25
John (total) = $75
Stinky = $25 ⎤ = $100

Summary
Performance income:

Performing right society pays John $50 as writer share.
Performing right society pays Stinky $50, which pays John 50%, or $25, and retains the same amount.

Other income:

Source pays Stinky $100. Stinky pays John $50 as writer (50/100, or 50%) and $25 as publisher (25/100, or 25%) while retaining $25 (25/100, or 25%).

Thus Stinky pays John 50% of performing income and 75% (50% + 25%) of other income.

4. **John is the sole writer and has a 50%/50% copublishing deal with Stinky Songs, which gets a 10% administration fee off the top.**

Mechanical, Synchronization, and Nonperformance Income

John (writer) = $45.00
John (publisher) = $22.50
Stinky (admin.) = $10.00
Stinky (publisher) = $22.50

John (total) = $67.50
Stinky (total) = $32.50
⎤ = $100

Public Performance

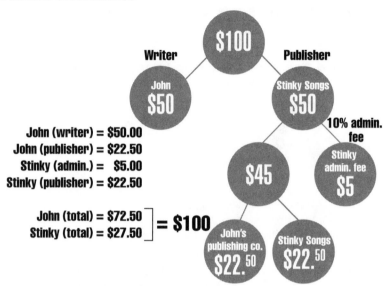

John (writer) = $50.00
John (publisher) = $22.50
Stinky (admin.) = $5.00
Stinky (publisher) = $22.50

John (total) = $72.50
Stinky (total) = $27.50 ⎤ = $100

Paid by the performing right society to the writer and, in this example, to Stinky, which administers 100% of the song. We are assuming that there is no contractual right to double the administration fee on the publisher's share of performance income.

Summary
Performance income:
Performing right society pays John $50 as writer share.

Performing right society pays $50 to Stinky. Stinky then pays $22.50 to John's publishing company (22.50/50, or 45%), retains an administration fee of $5 (5/50, or 10%), and retains $22.50 (22.50/50, or 45%) as its publisher share. Note that 45% + 45% + 10% = 100%.

Other income:
Source pays $100 to Stinky. Stinky pays $45 to John as writer (45/100, or 45%) and $22.50 as publisher (22.50/100, or 22.5%), or $67.50 (67.5%) total, while retaining $32.50 (32.50/100, or 32.5%).

Thus Stinky pays John 45% of performing income and 67.5% of all other income.

5. John is the sole writer and has a 75%/25% copublishing deal (in his favor) with Stinky Songs.

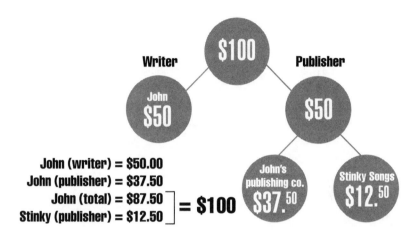

John (writer) = $50.00
John (publisher) = $37.50
John (total) = $87.50
Stinky (publisher) = $12.50 ⎦ = **$100**

Summary
Performance income:
Performing right society pays John $50 as writer share.

Performing right society pays Stinky $50 as the 100% administering publishing company. Stinky then pays John's publishing company $37.50 (37.50/50, or 75%) and retains the remaining $12.50 (12.50/50, or 25%).

Other income:
Source pays $100 to Stinky. Stinky pays $50 to John as writer (50/100, or 50%) and $37.50 as publisher (37.50/100, or 37.5%), or $87.50 (87.5%) total, while retaining $12.50 (12.5%).

Thus Stinky pays John 75% of performing income and 87.5% of all other income.

6. John and Bill are each 50% writers. John kept his publisher share, but Bill has a 50%/50% copublishing deal with Stinky Songs.

John (writer) = $25.00
John (publisher) = $25.00
Bill (writer) = $25.00
Bill (publisher) = $12.50

John (total) = $50.00
Bill (total) = $37.50   = $100
Stinky = $12.50

Summary
Performance income:

Performing right society pays $25 to John as writer share and $25 to Bill as writer share.

Performing right society pays John's publishing company $25. Performing right society pays Stinky $25. Stinky then pays $12.50 (12.50/25, or 50%) to Bill's publishing company while retaining $12.50 (12.50/25, or 50%).

Other income:

Source pays John's publishing company $50. John (as the publisher) sends half to himself as songwriter (he really doesn't have to do this) and retains the rest as publisher share.

Source pays Stinky $50. Stinky pays Bill $25 (25/50, or 50%) as his writer share plus $12.50 (12.5/50, or 25%) as his publisher share. Stinky retains $12.50 (12.5/50, or 25%). Note that Stinky pays Bill a total of $37.50 (or 75% of its receipts) and retains $12.50 (or 25% of its receipts).

7. **John wrote 80% of the song and Bill wrote 20% of the song. They agreed to give half of the publishing money to the film company that was using it as a major motion picture opening title song. Of the remaining half of the publishing, John had a 50%/50% copublishing deal with Stinky Songs, and Bill had a 75%/25% copublishing deal (in his favor) with Stinky Songs.**

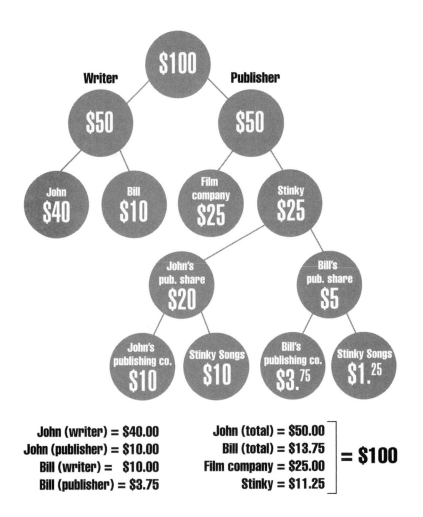

John (writer) = $40.00
John (publisher) = $10.00
Bill (writer) = $10.00
Bill (publisher) = $3.75

John (total) = $50.00
Bill (total) = $13.75
Film company = $25.00
Stinky = $11.25

$= $100

Summary
Performance income:

Performing right society pays John $40 (80% of $50) and Bill $10 (20% of $50) as writer shares.

Performing right society pays film company $25, or 50% of the publisher share.

Performing right society pays Stinky $25, which pays $10 to John's publishing company (10/25, or 40% of receipts) and $3.75 to Bill's publishing company (3.75/25, or 15%) while retaining $11.25 (11.25/25, or 45%).

Other income:

Film company collects $25 (we assume that the contract is such that the film company does not collect any writer share of income).

Stinky collects $75 and pays John $40 (40/75, or 53.3%) as writer, and $10 (10/75, or 13.3%) as publisher. Stinky pays Bill $10 (10/75, or 13.3%) as writer, and $3.75 (3.75/75, or 5%) as publisher. Stinky retains $11.25 (11.25/75, or 15%). Note that 53.3% + 13.3% + 13.3% + 5% + 15% = 100% of Stinky's receipts.

Glossary

Ad card: A little "MTV-type" notice within an advertising use, often in smaller type at the bottom of the screen identifying the name of the song and the group. Also called a chyron. Ad cards are often given for promotional value to compensate for a lower-than-normal fee.

Administration: The handling of all the day-to-day functions of a music publisher, such as (but not limited to) registering copyrights, clearing songs with performing right societies, negotiating and issuing licenses, collecting and reviewing royalties, and accounting and paying out royalties to writers, publishers, and other authorized participants.

Aggregate mechanical cap: To limit their maximum liability for mechanical royalties on a given album, record companies get artists to agree that the company will not be liable for royalties that exceed the amount earned by a given number of songs, or otherwise a fixed amount in dollars and cents. For instance, if you and the record company agreed to an aggregate mechanical cap of "12 songs at the minimum statutory rate at the date of initial release," then the record company is protected against your turning in an album with 52 songs on it (each 15 seconds long) and having to pay you 52 times the statutory rate.

Artist royalty: What the record company pays you to be a recording artist (i.e., as a musician or singer). Sometimes called a recording royalty. This does not relate to your songwriting or composing, which is covered separately by the payment of mechanical royalties.

Black box income: In many territories, the performing or mechanical right societies put all of the uncollected and/or unallocable income earned in their territories into a so-called black box account. This money is alternatively referred to as copyright control or suspense income. When copyright control or suspense income remains unclaimed for a specified (but varying by territory) period of time, the money "goes black box" and is then divided up among everyone else who earned money from that source. It's like dividing up extra spoils.

Blanket license: A license for an entire repertoire, instead of licensing on a song-by-song basis. For example, a TV station obtaining a blanket license from ASCAP gets to publicly perform every song in the ASCAP repertoire, and doesn't have to ask for permission to perform a given ASCAP song each time.

Bonus records: *See* free goods

Broad rights license: A comprehensive license form that covers just about everything the licenser can think of. This is opposed to a specific, limited license. For example, a broad rights synchronization license might cover TV, in-context advertising, motion picture theatrical rights, and home video devices. A TV sync license would only cover TV broadcast.

Bump: A performance or milestone bonus. A low-budget synchronization license might have bumps specifying additional payments to the publisher when a film attains box office receipts of $5 million, $10 million, etc. A deal that has bumps is referred to as a step deal.

Buyout: A deal based not upon a royalty per unit but upon a fixed agreed fee. A buyout license can be for the life of a song's copyright (plus renewals and extensions, if any) or for a fixed period of time. For example, you can grant someone a five-year video buyout in which he can use your song on as many concert DVD videos as he can sell within that term.

Catalog: An aggregation or collection of musical songs. For example, the Sea of Tunes catalog includes most of the big hit songs written by Brian Wilson and the Beach Boys.

Central licensing: A European mechanical licensing model whereby records are manufactured in one sole country within the European Union. For example, Universal Music might elect to manufacture and centrally license all of its CDs in the Netherlands, rather than duplicating function and effort by manufacturing in the Netherlands, Germany, France, Italy, Spain, England, etc. Centrally licensed and paid mechanical royalties are then paid out by the central licenser to each society within each European Union country in which the records are ultimately distributed.

Chyron: *See* ad card

Circular: A pamphlet on a given topic.

Co-administration agreement: An agreement between writers and/or publishers that specifies the writer and publisher shares, and who is responsible for the administration of the work.

Compulsory license: Generally, a license that is automatic and for which a publisher's explicit permission is not needed. With respect to phonorecords, this is a license that a record company obtains automatically as long as it complies with the compulsory license provisions of the copyright law.

Controlled: Refers to a writer, publisher, or song that is subject to a controlled composition clause.

Controlled composition clause: A clause (often very long and specific) within a recording agreement that specifies an agreement between the recording artist and the record company for songs that the artist writes, cowrites, or desires to record. In general, the controlled composition clause greatly cuts back on the liabilities and costs to the record company for mechanical royalties compared to what it would otherwise have had to pay under copyright law.

Copublishing: An arrangement in which one or more writers or publishers have a stake in a given work. In a copublishing deal, a writer typically assigns half of his copyrights to a music publishing company in exchange for monetary or other benefits. A copublishing deal may also be described as selling half of your publishing ownership and usually all of your administration rights.

Copyright: Ownership of intellectual property such as songs, software, books, and paintings, and the legal rights attendant thereto.

Copyright royalty: Usually (in the context of this book) refers to the fees to be paid for the use of a composition, as opposed to the fees to be paid as artist royalties.

Copyright control: *See* black box income

Cue sheet: An (often multipage) listing of all the songs appearing in a given film or TV show, showing all the music titles incorporated within the work, including other information such as the composers, the publishers, the type of use, the length of use, shares of ownership, etc. Performing right societies use cue sheets to determine who is to be paid for the performance of the music when a film or TV show that includes the music is publicly performed. It is crucial that publishers/writers verify the information listed on the cue sheet for any film or TV show that uses their music, and ensure that the appropriate performing right societies have received the cue sheet.

Derivative work: A work that is based upon or incorporates elements of a previously copyrighted work. Sampling or the creation of a medley may result in a derivative work. In general, permission of the owner of material incorporated into a derivative work is required under strict penalty of law. An unauthorized derivative work is an infringement, or a violation, of copyright law. If willful or intentional (as opposed to "accidental"), this unauthorized use is a felony.

Digital phonograph delivery (DPD): Delivery of a master recording by electronic means, such as via the Internet. Often this is in the form of an MP3 format electronic file. This is different from when you buy a physical product at a record store, but for mechanical licensing and royalty purposes, DPDs are usually treated the same as physical phonorecords.

Direct performance license: A license used when someone who will publicly perform copyrighted works (whether or not for profit) negotiates a license directly with the copyright owner (the publisher) instead of with a performing right society. Songwriter/publisher agreements with most performing right societies permit affiliated publishers to directly license works for performance to end users as long as they notify the societies.

DPD: *See* digital phonograph delivery

Employee for hire: The creator of a work for hire. *See* work for hire

Employer for hire: The party that commissions a work for hire. *See* work for hire

Ephemeral use: A transitory, nonpermanent use of a work. A typical example is a TV broadcast of a marching band in a parade performing a copyrighted song. The broadcaster had no way of knowing the song would be performed or broadcast and is generally not held liable for failing to prelicense this ephemeral synchronized use.

Exclusive: A type of agreement or use whereby all other parties are precluded from making a similar use. An exclusive advertising license with Coca-Cola gives Coca-Cola the sole right to use your song in commercials. A nonexclusive synchronization license to use your song in *Rocky 37* allows you to license your song to other films.

Fair use: Types of uses for which no license or permission is needed. Fair uses, for example, may be for educational, critical, or other free speech purposes.

Film festival license: Generally a limited, short-term, theatrical license, whereby a song can be synchronized in a film for a low fee and publicly performed in film competitions and the like. A publisher is under no obligation to grant or permit a film festival license.

Fix: The process of recording the details of a composition in a tangible media. Examples would be writing down a song as sheet music or recording it onto a cassette.

Fixed medium: The medium in which a work has been fixed: for example, sheet music or a cassette.

Free goods: Records that are (in theory) given to stores to entice them to order large quantities of records. A typical free good offer might be, "If you order 85 records, we'll send you 100." Stores also sometimes can get bonus copies to sell under other various promotional schemes.

In-context use: Use of a song apart from the work in which it was originally included that maintains the same linear synchronization that it had within the original work. For example, if your song is shown over three scenes of a birthday party in a film, and then those three scenes are aired on TV when an actor appears on *Letterman* to promote the film, and your music is used in the exact same manner as it was in the film, the use is in-context. An example of an out-of-context use is if your song from that film is used as a musical bed for a commercial advertising the film in which many scenes (but not the three that the song was originally synchronized with) are shown. It is typical (but not required) in a broad rights synchronization license to give in-context promotional uses, but to reserve (and thus license separately for an additional fee) out-of-context uses.

Joint work: A work created by two or more authors who intend their individual contributions to be merged into a new whole work. A newly cowritten song is a joint work. A famous poem set to music is a derivative work.

Linear: Used to describe a nonvariable one-to-one correspondence of sound and picture. Used when describing in-context uses. *See* in-context use

Long-song rate: U.S. copyright law specifies additional statutory mechanical payments for songs greater than 5 minutes in length. If the performance runs longer, you get paid more.

Master license: The license of a particular artist's recorded performance. A master license does not include the right to use the underlying musical composition, which must be licensed separately from the publisher (copyright owner).

Mechanical license: The license to use a song for phonorecords. This is for the right to use a composition, not for the right to use a given master recording (which is covered by the master license). Mechanical licenses are audio only, and do not cover synchronized uses with pictures as in films, TV programs, or videos.

Mechanical royalty: The royalty payable to the publisher (owner of the song) for a mechanical license. Usually specified in the United States as so many cents per copy made and distributed (even if not sold).

Mechanical royalty pool: The royalty pool established by a record company in conjunction with an aggregate mechanical cap. For example, a record company might negotiate a contract with a recording artist whereby the record company funds a mechanical royalty pool of $1 per album in connection with an aggregate mechanical cap. This $1 per album would first be allocated to the publishers of noncontrolled songs, and then the remaining pool would be spent on all the remaining controlled songs. *See also* aggregate mechanical cap, controlled

MFN: *See* most favored nations

Min-max: A type of controlled composition clause in which the record company is assured of a maximum aggregate mechanical payout and thus has its costs contained, and the artist (publisher in this case) has correspondingly gotten the record company to agree that if the aggregate mechanical costs are less than it agreed to pay, he receives the difference as a minimum. For example, if a record company has agreed to pay for ten songs per album on a "min-max" basis and the artist/writer puts 12 songs on the record, each song is paid at 10/12 of the agreed rate. On the other hand, if the artist/writer puts only eight songs on the record, he is paid 10/8 of the agreed rate for each song. In effect the artist says to the record company, "I'll help you contain your costs, but if there's extra left over from your budget, I get it."

Moral rights: Per the Berne Convention, "Independently of the author's economic rights, and even after the transfer of the said rights, the author shall have the right to claim authorship of the work and to object to any distortion, mutilation or other modification of, or other derogatory action in relation to, the said work, which would be prejudicial to his honor or reputation." In plain English, moral rights mean that even if you sell your work, you still have certain rights that survive the sale. The buyer cannot distort, mutilate, or modify the art you have created just because he owns it. Moral rights are troublesome, for example, to film studios, which want the right to distort and modify a director's or editor's work for such things as editing length or content for TV showings. Countries that are signatory to the Berne Convention afford their creators moral rights and greater protection of their art and reputation than nonsignatory countries.

Most favored nations (MFN): A clause in a contract assuring that no other contracting or licensing party is being treated more favorably or with better material terms. For example, if you license your song to a video project for "10 cents per unit sold on an MFN basis," and then the licenser agrees to pay the Rolling Stones 14 cents per unit sold, you are guaranteed to get the same rate the Rolling Stones got, which is the highest rate the producer is paying.

Music publishing: Generally, the ownership of the rights to a musical composition (and not the printing of sheet music).

Name, image, and likeness (NIL): The right, separate and apart from the use of a composition, to use the author's name, image, signature, or likeness in conjunction with a product. For example, a sheet music company that has licensed the right to use your songs in a songbook might also want to license NIL rights so it can use a photograph of you on the cover of the book.

Negative pickup: A film deal in which the film is made independently, and then a studio or distributer obtains (picks up) the right from the original producer to distribute the film (the finished negative).

Net publisher share: The amount a publisher retains after paying all third party royalties, such as songwriter and any publisher participant royalties. This is like net profit for the music publisher.

Noncontrolled: Not subject to a controlled composition clause. Usually a noncontrolled writer/publisher is a cowriter who is not part of the recording artist, or is the publisher of an outside song such as a cover recording. *See* controlled composition clause

Nonexclusive: Not exclusive. *See also* exclusive

Nonsurveyed performances: Public performances that are not monitored by performing right societies. For example, the ABC television network is monitored, and the results of the monitoring are used to allocate and distribute money that organizations like ASCAP collect. Nonsurveyed performances are at places like Mo's Bar on the corner. Your song might be played a lot at Mo's, and Mo might have an ASCAP license, but ASCAP isn't monitoring (surveying) performances at Mo's to see who it (ASCAP) should pay.

Out-of-context use: Use taken out of context from its original synchronization. *See* in-context use

PA and PAu copyrights: Copyrights for the performing arts. PA copyrights cover songs as well as dramatic works, scripts, pantomimes, choreography, motion pictures, and other audiovisual works. PAu is the designation given to unpublished (not yet publicly distributed) works of the performing arts.

Parody lyrics: In music publishing vernacular, parody lyrics are not necessarily lyrics that humorously mock the originals, but may be lyrics rewritten to fit the situation. For example, changing the line "Sweet little rock 'n' roller" to "Boy, I like Coca-Cola" would be considered creating a parody lyric. Parody lyrics in this sense must be approved by the original publisher and almost always command a premium over a licensed nonparody use. A true parody use may also be a fair use.

Penny rate: A royalty rate fixed in dollars and cents, rather than expressed in a percentage. For example, in relative terms, you might get 14% of the suggested retail selling price. In penny rate terms, your agreement might state that you get a flat $2.25 per CD sold. U.S. statutory mechanical rates are fixed as penny rates (currently 8.5¢ if the song is under 5 minutes in length) while foreign mechanical rates are often expressed as percentages.

Performance royalty: A royalty paid for the public performance of a copyrighted work. In most instances, performance royalties are paid by a performing right society but may be negotiated and paid directly between the user and publisher. Performance royalties are split into writer shares (50%) and publisher shares (50%) by the performing right societies.

Performing right society: Organizations that license public performances on behalf of music publishers, and then pay them royalties for the licensed performances. In the United States, the main performing right organizations in order of decreasing size are ASCAP, BMI, and SESAC. Most performing right societies throughout the world are either nonprofit corporations (in the U.S., operating under consent decree court supervision) or government controlled.

Per-program license: In lieu of getting a blanket license to publicly perform a performing right society's entire repertoire, some users of music opt to pay on a per-use basis. With a per-program license, they apply and pay for a public performance license to use only the music embodied in their programs.

Phonorecord: According to the United States copyright law, "material objects in which sounds, other than those accompanying a motion picture or other audiovisual work, are fixed by any method now known or later developed, and from which the sounds can be perceived, reproduced, or otherwise communicated, either directly or with the aid of a machine or device."

Preferred price to dealers (PPD): A term used mostly in Europe to describe an amount to which a royalty rate is applied. PPD is somewhat arbitrary but is closely akin to the wholesale selling price paid by a majority of retailers for a product. Mechanical rates per album in many European countries are 9.09% of PPD.

Prima facie: Evidence in a case or claim that is sufficient to establish it as truth in the absence of further facts or proof.

Professional manager: A music publisher's employee whose job it is to attempt to secure desirable licensing activity for the publisher's songs. Professional managers contact and visit record producers, film music supervisors, advertising agencies, etc., and try to convince them to use the publisher's songs. An older term is song plugger.

Promotional records: Records given away for promotional purposes. In general, artists and publishers are not paid for promotional records, which are usually marked "not for sale" and drilled or cosmetically disfigured to prevent them from being sold as new product. Promotional records are different from free goods, which are intended to be sold. *See also* free goods

Publisher half: Traditionally, the writer and the publisher have split all income on a 50%/50% basis. These roles have changed and in most cases today the writer is also the publisher, but the concept of splitting all publishing income into writer and publisher halves has persisted.

Recording royalty: *See* artist royalty

Recoupable: Describes any money advanced to you or on your behalf that will be recovered from your future earnings. Typical recoupable costs to a recording artist are advances, recording costs, video costs, equipment funds, producer fees, etc., which are recouped against your artist royalties. Publishing income (including mechanical royalties) is not recoupable against anything unless you have specifically agreed that it will be.

Rest of world (ROW): Publishing deals often carve out certain territories, and what is left after the carving is the ROW. For example, if you self-administer your publishing rights for the United States and Canada but plan to hire someone to administer and collect elsewhere, you are seeking a ROW deal.

Rights: There are many different and highly specific types of licenses a publisher may agree to. These licenses cover different rights, such as the right to synchronize, publicly perform, make phonorecords, or create advertisements using a given song.

Right holders: Synonymous with copyright owner. Within the context of this book, right holders are music publishers (with respect to owning the copyrights to songs) and record companies (with respect to owning master recordings).

Ringtone: An electronic sequence of songs or notes that play when a cell phone is called. The licensing of songs by music publishers for ringtones now generates more than $3 billion per year throughout the world. Ringtones may be monophonic (a single-tone melody), polyphonic (chords and melody), and "tru-tones" (actual master recordings, such as the Doors' "Hello I Love You"), and may or may not be combined with special graphics or screen animation.

Sampling: The use of other copyrighted material to create a new work. Samples may be of compositions and/or master recordings, and may be authorized or unauthorized (in which case the sample constitutes copyright infringement).

Song plugger: *See* professional manager

Songwriting deal: A business deal that pays you to write songs for the additional benefit of a third party. There are many types of songwriting deals, such as agreements in which a publisher owns your songs and pays you a royalty, copublishing deals (where you are partners of sorts), and work-for-hire agreements.

Split: Shorthand for how money or ownership is divided. A "50%/50% split on writing" means that you are a half writer and your partner is a half writer. Splits can be quite complex.

SR copyright: A sound recording copyright; that is, a copyright in the audio recording of a specific performance. This is the copyright for a master recording and does not necessarily cover the copyright in the underlying composition, which may be owned by a third party. *See also* PA copyright

Statutory rate: The U.S. mechanical rate for the reproduction of a composition on phonorecords as determined by law (or statute). Current (from 2004 until 2006) United States copyright law specifies a statutory rate for a song less than 5 minutes in length of 8.5¢ for each copy manufactured and distributed.

Step deal: A synchronization deal that involves bumps, or additional back-end payments predicated upon certain levels or milestones to be reached by the licenser. *See* bump

Subpublisher: A third party licensee who acts in the place and stead of the original publisher within a foreign territory. Most subpublishing deals have detailed specifications and terms that limit what a subpublisher can or cannot do without the original publisher's permission. Terms of subpublishing deals vary substantially as to how the subpublisher is compensated, the length of time of the agreement, and other significant terms. These days subpublishers provide services but do not obtain an ownership interest, although foreign ownership rights were sometimes transferred in very old subpublishing deals.

Suspense income: Income that is held (usually by a performing or mechanical right society) pending a determination as to who is entitled to claim it. Unclaimed suspense income will become black box money after a period of time that varies by territory. *See* black box income

Synchronization or sync license: A license relating to the synchronization of a musical composition in fixed timed relation with video images. Example: the use of a song in a film or TV program.

Synchronization royalty: The royalty paid for a synchronization license. In many cases, a synchronization use is paid by a flat fee covering a given set of rights for a fixed period of time. In some cases, there may be a royalty. An example of a synchronization royalty is the use of a song in a concert DVD video that is payable based on the number of units sold. *See also* video buyout

Tangible medium: Some sort of medium upon which information may be stored, such as paper, tape, or computer discs. In order to qualify for a copyright, a song must be fixed in a tangible medium from which it can be subsequently reproduced.

Video buyout: A fixed fee license for video synchronization. The opposite of a royalty-based deal. *See also* buyout

Video mechanical: A term sometimes applied to royalty-based deals (as opposed to a flat-fee video buyout) covering synchronization royalties for home video devices. The video mechanical may be based upon a percentage of something (such as the video selling price) or more typically as a penny rate per unit distributed.

Work for hire: A work created under the scope of employment in which the creating author is compensated but is not considered either the legal owner or author. In a work-for-hire situation (and in the rather restricted copyright type that results from it) the commissioning (or hiring) party is the legal author and owner. If you write a work for hire for Coca-Cola to be used as a new jingle, the company is legally the owner and writer of the song, and other than your fee (and whatever other consideration Coke agreed to give you), you get nothing else.

Writer half: Traditionally, the 50% of publishing income belonging to the writer. *See* publisher half

Index